# Praise for *eMarketing Strategies for the Complex Sale*

"In her outstanding book, Ardath Albee outlines a step-by-step process to help any business successfully engage its online customers and prospects. Her book is packed full with examples of how others have successfully attracted high-value prospects using creative online marketing tactics. If your business sells complex products or services, *eMarketing Strategies for the Complex Sale* is your guide book to attracting valuable prospects and speeding the sales cycle."

—Michael A. Stelzner, author of *Writing White Papers: How to Capture Readers and Keep Them Engaged*

"Albee, the quintessential marketing storyteller, reveals her secrets for developing exceptional content that will engage and nurture prospects from first engagement through the pipeline. If you want to be a better B2B marketer, read *eMarketing Strategies for the Complex Sale*."

—Christopher Doran, Vice President, Marketing, Manticore Technology

"If you're looking for 'eMarketing for Dummies' keep looking. This is not a simplistic overview. If you're looking for a comprehensive, well-researched, single resource to plan, build, execute and succeed in your eMarketing efforts, then buy this book! Ardath Albee knows her stuff and has packed it all into this dense but readable and usable text."

—Barry Trailer, Founding Partner, CSO Insights, www.csoinsights.com

"*eMarketing Strategies for the Complex Sale* is about getting the right content in the hands of the right people, at the right time, using the right medium to make the content truly relevant. Ardath Albee knows how to think like a prospect and translate this into how your business should respond to get their interest. This book is a must have for the Web 2.0 marketer."

—Mike Pilcher, VP Sales and Marketing at Marketbright and author of *Prosultative Selling*

"With *eMarketing Strategies for the Complex Sale*, Ardath Albee builds a compelling case for rethinking marketing from the perspective of the buyer. With engaging examples and actionable frameworks, she lays out a path to understanding buyer personas, building their trust, and delivering contagious content that they want to read. A must-read for B2B marketers looking to engage with today's buyers."

—Steven Woods, CTO, Eloqua and author,

*Digital Body Language*

"It used to be so darned easy: Do a few tradeshows, maybe publish a white paper or two, and have the salespeople follow-up. But the always on, YouTube-infested, Twitter-centric world makes the B2B sale much more complex today. Ardath Albee shows how smart business-to-business marketers learn about buyers, tell a story, and greatly influence the B2B lead-to-sale process, driving significant new business as a result. If you manage a complex sales process, stop making excuses! *eMarketing Strategies for the Complex Sale* is your guide for Web marketing success."

—David Meerman Scott, bestselling author of

*The New Rules of Marketing & PR* and *World Wide Rave*

"Ardath Albee gets it right in *eMarketing Strategies for the Complex Sale*. Albee puts you in the shoes of today's buyer and walks you through a fundamentally new buying process that is controlled by the buyer. Albee shows how marketing can nurture these buyers with contagious 'buyer focused" content that attracts and facilitates trusted conversations mapped to the buyer's readiness. A compelling read for both B2B marketing and sales professional alike, "eMarketing Strategies" is a practical and insightful how-to guide that will enable marketers to drive sales conversions and faster sales results."

—David Thompson, CEO, Genius.com and

founder of the Sales 2.0 Conference

New media, content marketing, social networking ... Ardath cleverly wraps these concepts in a bow and makes this book required reading. We are definitely not in Kansas anymore, so hold on to this book for dear life. If you do, you'll learn that it's not selling harder, it's selling smarter. Become the expert resource for your customer and watch your business grow.

—Joe Pulizzi, coauthor of *Get Content Get Customers*,

and founder of Junta42

# eMARKETING STRATEGIES FOR THE

# COMPLEX SALE

### ARDATH ALBEE

New York   Chicago   San Francisco   Lisbon   London
Madrid   Mexico City   Milan   New Delhi   San Juan
Seoul   Singapore   Sydney   Toronto

1 2 3 4 5 6 7 8 9 0   DOC/DOC   0 1 3 2 1 0 9

ISBN 978-0-07-162864-8
MHID      0-07-162864-9

This publication is designed to provide accurate and authoritative information in regard to the subject matter covered. It is sold with the understanding that neither the author nor the publisher is engaged in rendering legal, accounting, or other professional service. If legal advice or other expert assistance is required, the services of a competent professional person should be sought.

> *—From a Declaration of Principles jointly adopted by a Committee of the American Bar Association and a Committee of Publishers*

McGraw-Hill books are available at special quantity discounts to use as premiums and sales promotions, or for use in corporate training programs. To contact a representative please e-mail us at bulksales@mcgraw-hill.com.

This book is printed on recycled, acid-free paper.

**Library of Congress Cataloging-in-Publication Data**

Albee, Ardath.
   eMarketing strategies for rhe complex sale/by Ardath Albee.
      p. cm.
   ISBN 0-07-162864-9 (alk. paper)
   1. Internet marketing.   2. Customer relations.   3. Selling—Computer network resources.
I. Title.
   HF5415.1265.A4126 2010
   658.8'72–dc22

                                                            2009016402

*To my husband, Louis M. Tribbett, who supports all of my wildest dreams becoming realities.*
*I'd also like to pay tribute to Travis. His family's gracious gift of organ donation has enabled me to live those dreams to the fullest. Bless all of you, always.*

# Contents

# PART II    Customer Consensus

# PART III    Natural Nurturing

## PART VI    Meaningful Metrics

# *Foreword by Jill Konrath*

I f I've said it once, I've said it a thousand times: Sales is really tough in today's business environment. This isn't a complaint; it's simply a statement of reality.

Many salespeople are really struggling. I know because as a sales strategist, I work with them every single day to improve their sales effectiveness. And I've personally faced some big sales challenges myself.

Several years ago, my two biggest clients came under pressure from Wall Street to deliver better earnings. Virtually all external consultants were let go in one fell swoop. My business teetered on the brink of extinction for way too long as I sought to redefine my offering and rebuild my client base.

I'd always been someone who excelled at prospecting. It was easy for me to quickly establish a personal connection with a decision maker at the same time I provided a valid business reason for meeting.

But what worked for me in the past was no longer effective. People rarely answered their phones, all calls rolled to voice mail, and no one wanted to talk to a dreaded salesperson.

Why should they? All the information they needed was available on the Internet with a simple Google search. And, as far as they were concerned, salespeople ate up their precious time—which had become their most precious commodity.

Yes, the game definitely had changed, and salespeople had to learn new ways to crack into corporate accounts. It was now taking salespeople between 8 and 12 contacts (via e-mail, direct mail, voice mail, or phone) before they reached a decision maker. In addition, every contact had to focus on the prospect's critical issues, strategic imperatives, or business objectives.

This was the new price of admission for sellers to get their foot in the door. It meant they needed to invest significant time in researching companies, crafting messaging, and implementing numerous account-entry campaigns simultaneously.

But was that the best use of their time? As a sales purist, I'd love to say that it was just plain good selling. And personally, I'd love to be out their speaking to sales organizations about how to do it more effectively. Yet, hard as I try, too many sellers will never be able to master the high-level skills required to make this happen or have the discipline to do it on a regular basis.

In the past few years, it's become blatantly obvious to me that

1. Traditional methods of sales prospecting are grossly inefficient.
2. New strategies were needed to shorten sales cycles and improve seller productivity.
3. By embracing new technologies and a thought-leadership mindset, companies could transform sales results.

These things aren't easy for me to admit. But the truth is that no matter how hard I work with my corporate clients to improve sales effectiveness, it's just not enough anymore.

In the past few years, a number of new marketing automation companies (e.g., Eloqua, Marketo, Genius, and HubSpot) have appeared on the horizon. From the moment I saw their technology and their own implementation of it, I knew this was the solution I was looking for.

Marketers now can drive the lead-generation initiative with their ability to attract the online seekers, provide them with high-quality information that addressed the challenges they were facing, and nurture the relationship until the prospects were ready to meet with a salesperson. Marketing even could tell the seller what the prospect had read on the Web site or in an e-mail, how long they'd spent reading it, and if they'd forwarded the piece to others.

I was drooling! This was exactly what sales needed. This perfect care and feeding of potential customers eliminated the time-consuming task from the sales force at the same time that it ensured the consistency and quality of the messaging. It freed the salespeople to do what they do best!

But there was still a missing link! Technology was only the enabler. Contagious content was the key. I'm not talking self-serving marketing pablum, now. Prospective customers want answers to their problems, ideas for achieving their goals, and information on how others are addressing the same challenges they face. If you give the "state-of-the-art, leading-edge" blather, they'll delete your message in no time flat.

There's only one person I know who understands this implicitly—Ardath Albee. I first met her about five years ago when she was the president of a young technology company that was struggling to go to market the "old-fashioned way." After hiring (and firing) three salespeople, she knew it was time to try something different.

That's when she started blogging as a way to demonstrate thought leadership in her market space. Ultimately, her passion for "getting inside the customer's head" and crafting customer-enticing content led her to set up her own consultancy in this emerging field—one in which she is the clear leader.

*eMarketing Strategies for the Complex Sale* offers fresh perspectives and lots of meaty how-to advice on how to catch your prospect's attention, amplify your e-messaging, increase urgency, and build a relationship online. It's exactly what marketing needs to focus on today in order to help the struggling sales organization.

Sales desperately needs marketing to take the lead and up the ante. No more "same old, same old." It's time for marketing to make a radical impact—and this book shows you how.

Jill Konrath is a noted Sales Strategist and the bestselling author of *Selling to Big Companies*.

# Foreword by Brian Carroll

The single biggest focus for most B2B marketers today is lead generation. But I find marketers often can get so wrapped up in driving lead activity that they forget it's about driving sales conversion.

When I ask most executives and marketers what salespeople need to sell, they say, "More leads." But I've found that salespeople actually don't want more leads; what they want is "more effective selling time." It's not about more activity. It's about helping your sales team achieve better results.

After working with hundreds of clients on lead generation programs and sales, I frequently hear this "sticking point." They often ask, "How do we advance leads when there is some interest but not an immediate need to buy?"

The real challenge is not in generating leads, but rather in genuinely connecting with prospects. It doesn't matter how many leads are generated if prospects aren't willing to listen to what you have to say next. This is where eMarketing can have a profound impact.

I learned this first hand when the tech bubble burst. My company, InTouch, did lead generation work for a huge concentration of clients who were tech-driven software companies. At the time, most tech companies were bombing due to conditions over which we had no control. In two months, our company revenue was cut by 60 percent after losing just three clients. Our largest three clients all had their budgets cut, and the people we sold to left those companies. We were part of that resulting fallout, the little guys that get hurt. It wasn't a fun time for most people in marketing services.

As I was thinking about how we'd get through this crisis, I remembered that my clients repeatedly told me that our value wasn't just in our services but in what they learned from us that helped them to improve their lead generation results.

Ironically, I had no budget to spend on lead generation. So I thought, "Why not teach our future clients what we've learned and add value before they even start looking for lead-generation and marketing services?"

So I culled through a huge number of lead-generation strategies and tactics, some we knew, some we tested, and we just started sharing them with our prospects. This is when I discovered lead nurturing.

Lead nurturing is all about having consistent and meaningful dialog with viable prospects regardless of their timing to buy. It's about building trusted relationships with the right people by being a relevant resource. It's not a salesperson calling up every few months to find out if a prospect is "ready to buy yet." It's about adding value to future customers and helping them understand that you understand their journey.

I knew that nurturing could help my sales team to sell better because they could now add value to each sales interaction by sharing useful and relevant ideas. No more sales follow-ups with boring or irrelevant, "I'm just calling to touch base" calls. Their focus now was to be a resource regardless of time frame to purchase and to add value on every call.

Initially, I started writing articles for online publication and then giving my salespeople talking points and e-mail templates with links to relevant articles so that they could use them in their follow-up conversations and prospecting.

In October of 2003, I heard about this thing called blogging. I thought, "Wow, there aren't a lot of B2B companies writing blogs now. Here's some white space. I can take what I learned from writing articles, educate a new audience with a new channel, and leapfrog other companies who aren't embracing this now." I wrote my first blog post as a simple experiment, and the name of the "B2B Lead Generation Blog" hasn't changed since.

The decision to develop, educate, and nurture our future customers and help my sales team sell has returned results many times. My blog quickly became the most read blog on B2B marketing and lead generation, and our company flourished and was listed as one of the fastest-growing private companies in the United States by *Inc.* Shortly after that, I was approached by McGraw-Hill to write *Lead Generation for the Complex Sale,* and I've been humbled by its success.

The purpose of B2B marketing ultimately is to help the sales team sell, and I believe that the real key lies in actively creating nurturing, trustworthy, and "edu-focused" communication with your potential customers. Someone who really understands this is Ardath Albee.

I first met Ardath five years ago when she was president of an up-and-coming technology company. Her company sold software to help her customers execute eMarketing programs. I was struck by her ability to "get inside her customer's head" and help customers with what they needed. Ardath knew the software was good, but she realized that her customers needed more than a software platform. What her customers really needed was an overall eMarketing strategy and the right content to use the software to its fullest potential and generate return on investment.

So Ardath started helping her customers create eMarketing strategies and content focused on the progression of the customers' buying process journey.

With her experience, Ardath started a blog to share what she was learning, and she quickly developed a big following with B2B marketers. She then decided to set up her own consultancy that focused on this new field of eMarketing and content that helps to intensify the customer's buying process from first contact to close.

Ardath is now the top expert I know in the growing field of eMarketing strategy and customer-centric content development. I've been privileged to work with Ardath on a number of client programs here at InTouch, where we developed eMarketing strategies and content that accelerate the customer buying process.

*eMarketing Strategies for the Complex Sale* will show you how to create and use online content and communication strategies to capture and hold the attention of your prospects. Ultimately, this is the degree of engagement necessary to help your sales team win sales and attract more prospects.

Brian J. Carroll is the CEO of InTouch, Inc. and the bestselling author of *Lead Generation for the Complex Sale.*

# *Acknowledgments*

First and foremost, I want to thank Jill Konrath for her encouragement and support, which helped me believe it actually was a rational decision to start my own company and pursue my passion for customer-focused eMarketing. She's been instrumental in persuading me to step out to the edge and take chances that have transformed my career. There's no one else like her!

I owe a huge amount of thanks to Rebel Brown for her extraordinary partnership with clients, her friendship, and her tireless feedback and suggestions for this book. Her expertise helped to shape this book beyond what I could have accomplished on my own.

Thanks to my clients, who've helped to prove that e-marketing strategies and contagious content deliver appreciable business value. Special thanks go to Navid Azadi, Jon Miller, Mike Volpe, Pam Casale, and Christopher Doran for their conversations and willingness to let me write about their stories. And thanks to Brian Carroll for his partnership and encouragement to think about what's coming next.

To all the bloggers and Twitterers who so selflessly share their insights and opinions, opening up conversations that dig beneath the surface—I thank you. You expand my thinking every day.

Thanks to my agent, John Willig, who convinced me there was a market for this book and then went out and made it so. And much gratitude to my editors, Donya Dickerson and Ron Martirano and everyone at McGraw-Hill for their support and efforts in bringing this book to life—it's been my pleasure to work with you.

Finally, for Mom and Dad, who always reminded me that I was *a woman of vast potential*—thanks! Hopefully I'm getting there.

# eMARKETING ESSENTIALS

eMarketing strategies help companies build trusted relationships that generate demand.

## Chapter 1

# Why eMarketing Is a *Big* Opportunity for Complex Sales

What are marketers to do when traditional marketing alone isn't producing the business results their companies need? What if you can double, or even triple, your company's results with the same marketing dollars you have today? Sound impossible? It's not.

But first, it's important to realize that the way your potential customers buy has changed. Prospects are now much better informed. Their ability to access information directly on the Web has changed their expectations about the value and content delivered by vendor communications. By the time they interact directly with your company, chances are they know almost as much about your products as your salespeople—maybe even more. They've talked with their peers and colleagues and checked out your company via online resources far beyond the controlled environment of your corporate Web site.

These changes in the way buyers buy present a powerful opportunity for marketers to incorporate eMarketing strategies into their marketing mix to expand the way they build relationships across all the stages of the buying journey. Trusted relationships are the prerequisite for complex purchase decisions. With buyers staying elusive longer, creating an eMarketing strategy to reach, attract, and engage them through digital content and communications is one of the most important ways you can help to build that trust. In return, your marketing programs will generate higher levels of qualified demand predisposed to purchase from your company.

In addition to e-mail communications, eMarketing can enable companies to create online conversations, assess digital behavior, build virtual engagement, and use their Web properties to create interactive experiences that attract the extended interest of prospective and current customers. To attract and keep the increasingly limited attention of prospects, marketers must figure out how to incorporate the evolving opportunities the Internet empowers for building relationships that shorten time to revenue. The right eMarketing strategy enables marketers to meet their prospects online as trusted experts, engaging and educating them with relevant and valuable information that leads to sales success.

Taking a look into the beginning of a typical prospect's day demonstrates the difficulty of catching your prospect's attention—and the imperative of "What's in it for me?" that must be addressed to build engagement.

> It's Monday morning. Jerry arrives at the office running late due to a traffic snarl, chugging a mocha latte. He empties his briefcase, taking a moment to glance through the presentation he finished polishing last night after the kids went to sleep. Jerry's looking forward to the strategy meeting this afternoon, confident that the executive team will respond enthusiastically to his new pipeline momentum program. Sitting at his desk, he boots his computer and clicks to download e-mail, pleasantly surprised at the appearance of only 182 e-mails waiting for his attention. Noticing he only has 15 minutes before his departmental staff meeting, Jerry starts scanning messages.
>
> His brain immediately starts processing information, looking for senders or subject lines that appeal to him either because they are known or because they hit on an immediate need he's got. Like all of us, Jerry searches for things that are relevant to him because of his current personal and professional values and requirements.
>
> Jerry's calendar flashes a reminder on the screen. He's down to 10 minutes before his first meeting of the day. Part of his mind starts reviewing this meeting's agenda, another part wonders if he'll make his son's soccer game this afternoon, and the rest of it sifts those e-mails trying to deal with the most important first, decide which are useful enough to hold onto, and delete the ones that don't grab his attention.

If you think your prospects don't follow the same experience, think again. It's probably a lot like yours.

To put the problem of company-focused messaging into context, take a look at these e-mail first sentences and Jerry's likely reactions:

"I wanted to share with you the success of our [company] program which allows marketers to tap an influential group of [company's] readers for product sampling and reviews."

*I don't know you. I don't know who your readers are or what they could mean for me.*

"[Company name] has spent years perfecting its product for small businesses, leading to awards for both the company and the product and attracting more than 40,000 customers."

*This is the first I've ever heard of you. So, if you've tried to get my attention before, it wasn't memorable.*
"If [Company name] has its way, every last one of us will be communicating with video as naturally and regularly as we now use e-mail and our phones, no matter what industry we work in."
*Good for you. So why should I care?*

Each of these first sentences is all about the company sending the message with no indication they recognize issues Jerry is working to solve and how they can help.

- There's no consideration evident about Jerry. He's a busy guy with issues to solve and a daily to-do list that never seems to shorten.
- There's no reason at all for Jerry to keep reading. Unless he's a fan of your company's information, what will engage him?
- There's nothing relevant to anything he's thinking about right now. He's got lots of top-of-mind responsibilities. These sentences don't set any expectations of helping him meet them.

All these e-mail openings are talking about the company that's sending them, not speaking with Jerry about his high-priority issues. Because these messages don't immediately engage Jerry, he deletes them. Talking about your company versus your prospects is status quo. It's evident in the content companies publish on corporate Web sites, microsites, blogs, and in social media exchanges.

Articles, reports, and research findings claim that e-mail effectiveness is declining or that e-mail is dead. Don't believe it. E-mail is a valuable marketing tool, as are the other modes of digital publishing that empower marketers to publish content in real time. eMarketing effectively provides information to all of us every single day—when it's done with us in mind instead of a company.

The reason response and engagement rates are not impressive isn't due to the technology or the delivery method. It's the lack of contextual stories that relate to your prospect's specific situations—their challenges, issues, and opportunities. To attract and engage prospects with your company, you've got to take the time to understand who your audience is and what they're interested in—and why. The better you know your buyers, the more interactions you can create that drive business results. Through current eMarketing techniques, companies are able to eliminate cold calling while achieving results such as 375 percent increases in qualified opportunities, 30 percent shorter time to revenue, and more.

## THE SHIFT TO SELF-EDUCATION

By all accounts, the sales cycle is lengthening. More people are involved in making the purchase decision, and each of them has less time. On top of this, innovation is changing the way business gets done faster than ever. Your prospects only have time to ingest new information that stands to impact a current, pressing priority. This is why they've taken control over the information they choose to access and use. They use their time to gain the specific knowledge they need to make confident purchase decisions. Being better informed means they can delay sales conversations until marketing has engaged them with valuable ideas that indicate your company can improve the outcomes they get from solving their problems.

Even as prospects are more informed, the growing complexity of their problems offers marketing an opportunity. By publishing content that shows buyers you understand their problems and can show them how to solve them, you build credibility. With consistent reinforcement that your content is continuously relevant to them, prospects will seek it out proactively. This self-education shift is an invitation to marketers to build better engagement by showing prospects that you've helped customers just like them solve their problems successfully.

The information buyers need is becoming more freely available online. And because of this, there's no longer a big advantage to opting-in to your marketing initiatives. Effective eMarketing strategies have shifted to focus communications to wherever a company's prospects spend time online. The point is now not to capture them, but to attract them. Instead of forcing them into your nurturing programs, use content to entice them to self-identify and ask for inclusion. Once your company is known for delivering valuable information, you'll find prospects readily seeking you out to grow a relationship.

However, in order to do this, you have to know your buyers really well. If you don't, someone who does will come along at any moment. Prospects respond when companies "hear" them. They don't have time to figure out how products suit their specific situations. The problem for your prospects isn't in finding products but in getting the outcomes they're tasked to deliver. To do this well, they need advisory vendors who are experts in delivering desired business outcomes. The sooner marketers adjust to the fact that prospects control the buying process, the more valuable marketing will become to your company.

## SIX THINGS TO CHANGE ABOUT YOUR CONTENT AND COMMUNICATIONS

Once marketers can put themselves into the shoes and perspectives of their customers, they'll gain higher engagement levels and increased credibility. The following six tips expose some of the most common missteps marketers make with their marketing programs. Incorporate these tips into your marketing, and you'll find your focus shifting naturally to your prospects and customers—instead of on your company and products.

### Feeds and Speeds

Marketing content that revolves around a company's products, features, and statistical outcomes without addressing the context of the prospect's specific situation is not valuable to today's prospects. Feeds and speeds don't affect your prospects unless you've helped them to visualize getting successful outcomes by using them and, of course, unless you've shown them that those outcomes solve the priority at the top of their to-do list.

### Preaching to the Choir

Instead of developing content from the perspectives of people inside your company, reach outside to embrace your prospects' perspectives.

For example, instead of talking about a new feature, share a story about why that feature helps prospects get something they need. Where you once would've discussed your solution, start a dialogue about the industry trend that increases the need for what your product does. Focus on generating dialogue interesting to your customers and people like them.

### Impersonalized Outreach

Inserting the first name of your prospect into an e-mail message is not personalization. A generalized message meant to serve everyone isn't relevant to most. To get personal, you need to focus communications on groups of people with similar interests. Segmentation, as a component of your eMarketing strategy, will help you focus the entire message and content offer on your prospects, not just the salutation. Content that promises to discuss a specific topic should do so, not serve as a thinly veiled sales pitch. Content published on industry-related Web sites must be shaped to serve the interactions happening in that venue. One-size-fits-all content is still the norm for today, and it serves no one well.

### The Fantasy of Control

People who may have never met each other in the past are now discussing your company and products online. Marketing now has the opportunity to step into conversations never before available, but only if they share in the discussion, not try to control it. You may have lost the ability to control the conversation, but by showing up in a context that is instantly relevant to your prospects, you've gained the ability to help shape those dialogues. Regardless of the spin you'd like to put on something, give it up. Instead, respond to people discussing issues with helpful information that attracts them to seek more.

### One-Off Messaging

Sending out messages based on the latest product management or executive whim is not an eMarketing strategy. It's a recipe for boring, even alienating your prospects. Many marketers fail to realize that content that's not consistent has no story—at least not one that compels your prospects to want to know more. An invitation to a Webinar about the capability of one product followed by a white paper download and then an inquiry about setting aside 15 minutes to chat about some other product doesn't build engagement. An eMarketing strategy designed to engage buyers from the beginning of their buying journey through purchase will help marketers deliver a compelling story their prospects want to spend time with because it's valuable to them.

### Fear, Uncertainty, and Doubt

Think carrot, not stick. We've established that your prospects are better informed. Painting gloom-and-doom pictures of failures they'll experience if they don't use your products and solutions will turn them off. Instead, develop content and communications that show you understand what they're facing and that you've helped other customers with the same issues solve their problems.

### OFFLINE VERSUS ONLINE

The truth about marketing is that someone has to respond to marketing content before you know it's had impact. The difference between offline and online marketing initiatives is that online marketers have more visibility into how people are responding. Marketers know who they're engaging, and what's being said regardless of whether or not prospects respond directly.

Marketing is in the curious position of interacting with a high volume of people they (mostly) never meet personally. Traditionally, marketing measured results with press clippings, direct-response mailers, and the vague circulation numbers stipulated by print publications. With eMarketing, marketers can gauge interest levels and assess a multitude of indicators—such as pass-along value, views of related content, and real-time comments. They can monitor interest expressed by audiences previously unknown to expand sales channels and reach influencers they aren't aware of.

All this said, there are similarities between online and offline marketing that should be noted. For example, content that flows freely across the Internet and is accessed by people who find it valuable is similar to TV exposure. Companies have spent a lot of money on television and radio without strict correlation with revenue. They spend these dollars to generate awareness, attract people to their products, and engage them with their brand. The more reach, the better, and the Internet expands this opportunity.

But many marketers are wary of allowing content to flow freely online. Just because marketers can gate content doesn't mean they should. In fact, given the information choices available today, it makes a lot of sense to go for the broadest reach and leverage your content to do the heavy lifting. Think about it this way: Instead of a 15-second spot, you can deliver valuable content that people will spend minutes reading. Smart marketers focus on making their content so engaging that readers forward links to their friends, post links on their blogs, and mention what's valuable about the content on social applications. With opt-in and hand-raising the new measures of demand generation, forcing the issue just isn't in your best interests. In fact, why would you want to spend precious time focusing on people who haven't demonstrated an interest in your products and services beyond knowledge transfer? Instead, marketers need to realize that each bit of knowledge prospects ingest from you builds your credibility and expertise with them for whenever the time comes that your products and services answer their needs. When that happens, prospects will happily opt in to learn more about how you can help them.

Online marketing presents unprecedented visibility, intelligence-gathering options, and distribution at rates previously unattainable. Using these benefits, marketers can take action to build trusted relationships that turn into customers.

## WHAT YOU NEED TO KNOW

eMarketing strategies for complex sales have lots of moving parts and require different ways of thinking than were used in interruptive-style marketing. This book is designed to serve as a complete guide to how to create eMarketing initiatives that establish strong connections with your prospects and customers, getting them to buy more often from your company as a result. You'll learn how to build the foundation that personalizes your marketing initiatives and how to engage buyers across the stages of their buying process with progressive nurturing programs. Beyond producing sales-ready opportunities that power faster and more profitable revenues, you'll also gain strategic insights about how to set up salespeople to win more often after the handoff to sales. And you'll see some methods for measuring the impact of eMarketing strategies as valuable components of your marketing mix that directly impact business results.

The sooner you start shifting toward embracing your customers' perspectives and developing high-value content that encourages dialogue, the faster you'll start reaping the rewards. And so will your prospects and customers.

## Chapter 2

# The Mutual Rewards of eMarketing Strategies

Marketing can become the driving force behind why your prospects actually make the choice to become your customers. The very nature of eMarketing calls on marketers to get closer to their customers by understanding what's important to them. And when your marketing is backed by a strategy designed to deliver business value, the farther you reach, the better the outcomes. Building online engagement also depends on your ability to develop compelling content. This is next to impossible if you don't write for an audience you understand. When you do, the rewards are plentiful.

*Engagement bling* is what I call the positive results your company gains from sustaining trusted engagement with prospects and customers throughout their buying journeys. The really great thing, though, is that it's not all just for you. Your prospects and customers also receive payoffs from your dedication to eMarketing strategies. And that makes a huge difference in the potential benefits—for both of you.

Let's take a look at the engagement bling for both you and your prospects and customers so you know what you're working toward accomplishing.

## REWARDS FOR YOUR COMPANY AND YOU

Building relationships through online interactions delivers value beyond the simple analytics of clicks and views. A complex sale takes a number of interactions to result in a purchase decision. Engagement bling swings the odds in your favor and shortens time to decisions.

### Interactive Dialogues

Interactive exchanges are what transform push marketing to attraction marketing that pulls more prospects into your pipeline. In the traditional push style, marketers broadcast their content to people they select without regard for relevance based on audience perception. The content is usually about the company and its products, followed by a sales offer. The marketing database is treated as a universal clump of as many people or companies the marketer can find that might have a need for the product the company sells—kind of like throwing stuff against the wall to see what sticks. Push marketers generally take the opt-out approach, making the assumption that unless their audience chooses to "unsubscribe," they want to hear from you. What happens when companies do that to you? You delete or unsubscribe and generally ignore messaging that wastes your time.

On the other hand, messaging that invites interactive dialogues entices prospects to make faster progress through their buying journey. With attraction marketing, marketers make it worth their prospects' time and effort to give their permission. Your prospects request to be included in your company's content delivery plan because they value the information the company provides. Attraction marketing invites such interactions as responses, feedback, comments, questions, and participation. All these activities can be designed to shorten the time-to-purchase decision. Given the increased trust created, prospects pass along referrals to your content, increasing your reach and attraction potential, pulling even more prospects into your marketing programs.

### Intelligence-Enhanced Listening

When your eMarketing strategy presents a planned, consistent delivery of high-value content focused on what drives your prospects and customers, you have the opportunity to communicate with them and learn more about their specific needs. By interrelating your content, each click deeper into the subject matter can be designed to gather intelligence about your prospects. You begin to learn not just that they like to do their research on Tuesdays but also about their interest levels, buying stage, and intention to take action to solve their problems.

Learning to listen to your prospects and customers by creatively designing how you gather intelligence pays off in big ways. If you compare the content your prospects and customers pay attention to with your content map for that topic, you can learn if you have gaps that should be filled. Additionally, you can learn if you've missed with your hyperlink wording, or misjudged what your prospects need based on their buying stage.

Content marketing is never perfect. The ways in which people gather and ingest information are continually evolving along with the nature of the problems they're solving. By enhancing your "listening" with gathered intelligence, you can discover a lot about what works—and what doesn't. Listening is a new skill for many marketers. It requires time, patience, and the ability to exchange your perspective with that of your prospects for the purpose of evolving meaningful interactions. Listening is likely to become the "secret sauce" for effective marketing in an increasingly interactive world that powers increased revenues and profits for your company.

### Increased Demand

The goal of marketing in a complex sale is to generate qualified demand that efficiently transitions to revenues. And if you want to increase the level of demand for your solutions, it is critical that you enrich the relationships your company establishes with prospects and customers. Marketing with contagious content operates like a pay-it-forward system for your company. This is because the value your content provides transfers to the value your prospects and customers ascribe to your company. Marketing is like a trial run from a prospect's experience perspective. The better the prospect's perception of the experience your content delivers, the higher the revenues in return.

Influencing the influencers pays you back by generating more conversations focused on your company's ideas and concepts. These conversations serve to aid in escalating the interest people have in your company's products through insights to your company's unique expertise. The more people talk to other people like them about your company's ideas, the higher the growth in demand, and the easier it is to gain consensus from the project team for a purchase decision.

### Higher Trust

Consistency in messaging, delivery, and perceived value all add to your company's credibility with prospects and customers. Once prospects trust you to deliver relevant and helpful content, they'll want to hear more from you and will anticipate working with your company. In addition, being able to apply personalization to improve the quality of relationships is more important than ever in influencing your prospects' buying decisions. According to the Edelman Trust Barometer 2008,[1] people say that they trust "people like me" more than any other source. When you show that you understand the problems and business realities they're facing, people can't help but talk about the valuable ideas you've shared with them and the insights you've provided.

With each positive interaction, their trust in your company will grow. Trusted advisors are much more valuable to prospects than vendors. People buy commodities from vendors. They buy expertise and outcomes from trusted advisors—which means higher and more profitable revenues. And they rely on them long term for continued success. Engagement is a critical component of gaining trust, and that trust is a prerequisite for purchase decisions.

## REWARDS FOR THEM (YOUR CUSTOMERS AND PROSPECTS)

Buyers are focused on the "What's in it for me?" when they search for ideas and insights. Rewarding them with engagement bling when they interact with your content encourages more of them to self-select your company and enter your pipeline.

### Valuable Knowledge

Your prospects need your help to learn how to best solve their problems. People are being asked increasingly to solve problems that are not within their core competency. They're already overloaded with work before they get this new responsibility. In fact, they're so busy that they don't have time to think strategically. For example, a recent survey of CIOs showed that only 10 percent of their time was spent on strategy; the rest was spent on tasks to keep things running smoothly. People need to acquire knowledge that helps them make the best possible decisions—for their companies as well as their careers. When the content you provide helps evolve how prospects approach problems and applies your solutions in ways that work based on their company's unique situation, they can visualize the valuable outcomes attainable from working with your company. People buy outcomes from vendors who understand their businesses.

### Increased Confidence

Well-executed interactive marketing gives prospects the confidence to reach out to vendors who engage them to validate the assumptions they've made while gathering knowledge. Beyond making the best choices in how they address problems or capitalize on opportunities, your prospects need the confidence to know they've selected a trusted advisor to help them execute projects that deliver the outcomes their businesses require. Buyers hesitate when they're unsure. If they have doubts that they're making the best choice, they tend to make no decision at all. And that outcome isn't good for anyone.

With the right eMarketing approach, prospect interactions grow engagement. With trust-based relationships, your prospects' confidence in your company's capabilities and the increased quality of their decisions grows.

### Useful Conversations

Engagement helps you to simplify complexity by establishing conversations with your prospects based on their needs. We all know that the buying journey is getting longer. Economic conditions are pushing the time it takes to establish the consensus required to make a decision. The complex nature of business problems, coupled with the opportunities for competitive advantage, makes the decision process unwieldy. With eMarketing focused on your buyers, not only are you sharing knowledge and building confidence, but you're also able to converse with them from their perspective about the specifics that interest them.

The best thing about conversations created through engagement is that your prospects often will initiate them on their own. This mindset is all about the prospect's desire to be in control of his buying process. With increasing levels of engagement, your company won't be sitting out on the crucial discussions you need to participate in to make the sale. In fact, with a solid eMarketing strategy, you'll have the opportunity to connect salespeople with prospects at that conversational point—seamlessly and fluidly—without missing a step. With conversations focused on providing the business value they need, buyers will make purchase decisions faster, without the need for protracted evaluations.

### *Higher Credibility*

As you nurture your prospects, providing relevant knowledge they need, helping them build their competence in new subject matter, and encouraging them to enter into conversations with—and about—your company, you're building credibility for them and for you. The very nature of an eMarketing strategy for the complex sale dictates that relevance, consistency, and value are inherent in every single interaction. With each impression designed to deliver on these factors, based on the perspectives of your prospects and customers, credibility grows.

Don't ever think that you're only nurturing your prospects to keep yourself at the top of their minds for whenever they decide to buy. Nurturing is as much about your company as it is about your prospects. Your credibility is strengthened by each valuable impression. As they reap the rewards of knowledge that builds their competence in solving their problems, your prospects are enabled to discuss their project objectives with clarity and confidence. This evolution in knowledge, built with your content, contributes to increasing their credibility with project stakeholders. Your intent to help them is clear and must remain pure and transparent. By following these guidelines, you'll see engagement pay off on both sides of the scale—for you and, most important, for them.

### SHAPING THE STORY

Engagement bling delivers some great rewards for your company. The way you choose to use your bling will determine just how big a part those rewards can play. But it gets even better. By integrating your rewards, you can raise the stakes by applying them to how you shape the continuous story your company is sharing. A consistent and coordinated eMarketing strategy uses integrated building blocks to communicate the overarching storyline you need to generate buy-in from your existing and future customers. This happens when you empower your audience to visualize the success made possible by harnessing your expertise, along with your product or service offerings.

When your words—whether audio, video, or textual—enable customers to step into your stories and see themselves solving their problems in a way that delivers the business value they need, you've got traction. Talk is cheap. This is evident every time you have an "About Us" company Web page or bio at the end of a press release that starts off with, "Our company is the leading provider of . . . . " People are immune to the inflated statements companies make about themselves. Even if the statements are true, your customers care only about how that information manifests in reality for them.

The more traction you have, the more power you have to shape (notice I didn't say *control*) the story around your company's promise delivery. However, this doesn't happen in a vacuum. You have to spread your content far and wide to intersect with your prospects and customers—and their peers—online. Until you're in the conversation, your stories won't have the traction they need to make a difference.

The mutual value derived from shaping stories is that the people who retell them by visualizing their futures will add to those stories. They'll share them with their colleagues, peers, and bosses. Your stories will take on a life of their own. Instead of just pushing content out, you need to be focused on pulling the threads people evolve back inside your company. They'll help you to continuously shape and develop new directions for your stories that meet the evolving needs of your customers.

You see, shaping also goes both ways. There's mutual value in the insights you help your prospects and customers understand, as well as the reciprocal value you receive when they put their own spin on them. To get the best results, you've got to start with the imperative to really and truly get to know your customers.

## PART II

# CUSTOMER CONSENSUS

To create sustainable and trusted relationships, companies need to thoroughly understand their customers and agree on the unique definitions for each market segment.

## Chapter 3

# Using Personas to Understand Your Customers

The core of eMarketing is based on a thorough understanding of and focus on your customers. Building engagement and becoming customer-centric are competencies companies must develop to ensure sustainable growth. Engagement is the willingness of prospects and customers to interact with your company at increasingly higher levels. According to the *Online Customer Engagement Report 2009*, 52 percent of companies say that customer engagement is essential, whereas another 35 percent termed it important. Interestingly, only 45 percent of companies say that they have a customer-engagement strategy.[1]

To develop eMarketing strategies that increase the win rate on complex sales, you've got to get closer to your customers. One way to establish the level of connectedness you need to create a progressive dialogue between prospects and your company is to employ personas. A *persona* is a composite sketch representative of a type of customer you serve. Personas extend beyond the traditional demographic profiles commonly used to summarize an ideal customer. They include job-situation details, responsibilities, and influences on buying decisions that bring the sketch to "life" for the purpose of creating more relevant, personalized communications. Personas transform the ways you think about and talk with your prospects and customers. Personas make the difference between interacting with a stranger and joining a relevant conversation. Narrowing your focus takes you from generalist to specialist as you share your expertise.

The concept of niche marketing is not new, but it's never been more important. The ideal relationship is one to one. This usually happens in sales, but it's difficult to create and sustain when marketing to a large roster of prospects. By focusing on a highly defined combination of personas and niches as the compass for your eMarketing strategies, you'll be able to noticeably increase prospect engagement levels.

Many companies today collect demographic information about their prospects and customers. The problem with stopping at demographics is that you're only using objective qualification metrics designed to help your company select markets. You've learned nothing about why or how those prospects may want to buy from you. Companies need to expand the information they gather about their prospects and customers to include behavioral and psychographic insights that help them fine-tune and improve their ability to create trusted relationships.

## CUSTOMER PROFILES—THE WIDE-ANGLE LENS

Let's say that you take a look at your prospect database and see 25,000 contacts. Beyond your largest customers, you might not have previously entertained the idea of thinking about those contacts individually. When I ask companies to define their prospects, they give me a demographic profile that includes decision-maker title, industry, and company size (whether by revenue or by number of employees) as the predominant characteristics. This profile doesn't focus on what's important to your buyers. They become a clump of data without human attributes. In B2B marketing for complex sales, often the image of the person companies are selling to is a flat, one-dimensional representation of a buyer. But this is just not true.

Most companies gather broad, company-based information about such things as their customers' overall place in the market (e.g., Fortune 500) and their industry (e.g., pharmaceutical or technology). Occasionally, they go a step further and supplement their records with ambiguous notes about company philosophy and cultural mores with observations such as high-growth, innovative, startup, dominant player, etc. While this type of broad perspective is a good start, it's got too much wiggle room in it to be helpful in directing your focus for eMarketing strategy development. For eMarketing to produce the best results, you need a laser focus on target segments, not a scattershot approach.

As an example, consider the confusion that can develop if you use broad industry definitions for your prospects. A technology company could be a hardware or software company. It could create solutions for consumers or for businesses. The company also could be a service provider that is an integrator or value added reseller (VAR) for another technology company. It could be a startup or a Fortune 100 company—or anywhere in between. The company's customers could vary widely, which means that its needs and situations could be completely different from another prospect in this same industry. Depending on the size and type of company, the prospect you target also may wear other hats within the organization that affect her perspective on a new problem she's charged with solving.

The whole point of a customer profile should be to generate insights about that prospect to help you understand why and how you can help her be more successful. When you show you understand the prospect—and her business—she will interact with you to learn more. A customer profile is best used as a foundational base from which to begin persona development and refinement.

For those of you who are unsure about why your company should invest the effort to master personas, consider the shift of power in the sales environment from your company to your customers. A customer profile is valuable because it gets your company to put a stake in the ground and select a direction—or several—to direct your efforts. Without it, your focus is too wide. The problem with the wide-angle approach is that there are just too many variables to address under one umbrella.

Trying to serve too wide an audience means you really serve no one well enough to add value. It's imperative for you to deeply understand what your prospects are interested in, the obstacles they're facing, and the outcomes they need. This is how you trump the alternative communications and content that hit your prospect's inbox, show up in search results, or are recommended by their colleagues and peers. Incorporating behavioral and psychographic insights with basic demographics enables communications to consistently deliver instantly recognizable value.

As further proof that profiles won't get you close enough to build trusted relationships, research shows us that there's a huge difference in perception between companies and their customers. Want proof? According to the CMO Council, 56 percent of companies believe they are customer-centric, and only 12 percent of their customers agree. When asked whether vendors are getting better at understanding and responding to customer needs, nearly 45 percent of customers answered "No" or "Not sure."[2] Given the increasing control of customers over their buying journey and their avoidance of your sales process, gaining a customer-centric perspective is definitely critical to future marketing success. And this is where personas come into play.

## WHY A PERSONA IS DIFFERENT FROM A PROFILE

Before we jump into talking about creating personas, let's talk about the beauty of a niche. After all, the best reason to use a segmentation strategy is because your company is in pursuit of prospects who occupy a particular niche. There are a number of advantages to using a niche-marketing mindset as you develop personas. By their very nature, niches prevent you from trying to push the boundaries of a persona into a diluted state because you want to expand your reach or, conversely, don't want to leave anyone out. Personas keep you focused on creating customer-centric connections. Your content and messaging will have increased relevance because they're about people like them—not everyone. If you want to expand your reach, choose another niche, and create another persona to go with it.

### The Beauty of a Niche

Employing niches in your marketing programs means that topics and ideas are more easily focused on your audience because you've reduced the amount of variables to address. A niche is defined with specific parameters. It's a slice of the whole picture where a subset of your prospects exists—those with a narrow focus of interest. Best of all, focusing on a niche enables you to go very deep within a buyer's circumstances and explore nuances related to his specific issues that wouldn't be seen as relevant to anyone outside that group.

A niche, by its very nature, catches the attention of those to which it appeals. These people are the ones who will go out of their way to participate and interact with it—as well as with others who have the same interests. You'll find it easier to generate relationships because the relevance of your communications and content will be so high that they will spawn interactions based on the establishment of a common foundation for dialogue. And a niche focus increases your prospects' view of your company as a specialist with the expertise they need. This is because you are perceived to be focused solely on them.

Think about the beauty (and the potential payoffs) of a niche. Niches come to life when you add personas. A persona takes a segment of your company's aggregate customer profile and fleshes it out with detailed information that represents real prospects in specific circumstances. The more specific you can get about the boundaries of your niche, the more your persona can become a viable representation of your prospective customers. Consider as a simple example of narrowing to a niche focus the idea that "all people who drive SUVs" is not the same market as "those who drive Hummers." And remember that a niche is different from a persona. One niche can have a variety of personas. You would market differently to female buyers of Hummers than to men who drive Hummers, for example. Or, a director of information technology will have different interests than a chief information officer.

B2B personas are a bit different from consumer personas. Consumer personas are focused exclusively on the person. Personal characteristics are important, but B2B personas must recognize that the prospect's professional standing and priorities will hold additional sway over what catches his attention when it comes time to solve a business issue. B2B persona information will vary but can include

- *Status quo*. Marketers need to look beyond just the issue their prospects are trying to solve and get a feel for their current professional situation. There are many reasons for an issue to arise as well as reasons it has yet to be solved. Political reasons may exist that keep the issue from being resolved. There may be a lack of consensus about how fixing the problem will help to achieve strategic objectives. Look for the obstacles that exist to keep your prospects from taking action. Addressing their current situation will help marketers demonstrate their understanding and increase relevance.
- *Strategic business and career goals*. For prospects to take action to resolve an issue, there must be a viable business outcome that helps to achieve the goals of their company. But your prospects are also interested in advancing their careers. They need to make the best possible decision for both their companies and their career

advancement. By learning more about what your prospects need to achieve—both personally and professionally—you'll gain insight about what matters most.

- *Preferences and aversions.* Just as there are a variety of reasons why a problem may exist, your prospects can be predisposed to how they will consider solving them. Depending on the industry and the business issue, your prospects may respond better to a particular perspective. Whether they favor the idea of taking advantage of an opportunity or mitigating risk, learning more about these predispositions can accelerate your ability to build engagement—and a trusted relationship.

- *Competitive considerations.* Many decisions about which priorities companies choose to solve are related to their place within their market. An outcome for solving an issue that enables better differentiation likely will get higher attention than one that simply mirrors what a competitor is doing. Researching industry trends can provide insights about competitive considerations.

- *Influencers.* During a complex sale, there are a number of influencers providing input and ideas about how to deal with a priority issue. Companies that focus on learning about who their prospects interact with during their buying process can expand their dialogues to engage these other players. Within a company, these influencers can be colleagues, stakeholders affected by the project's objective, employees (end users), and champions. Externally, your prospects will talk with their peers and consult with industry analysts and other experts.

## CREATING PERSONAS

The best way to wrap your mind around a B2B persona is to take a look at one. Let's take a look at the fictional persona of Gloria.

> Gloria is the manager of product development for the Whiz Bang 3X product at a midsize technology company. She's three months from the product's launch and has the weight of the company's belief—that this product will be critical to their future success—riding on her shoulders. She's working 18-hour days and has just discovered that the delivery

system the product team had selected isn't going to be able to scale to meet projected volume needs.

Gloria's status quo is that her company is conservative and generally moves slowly. The company has taken a big risk on the Whiz Bang 3X and has reached its tolerance for stepping out to the edge. No one is willing to stick his neck out much farther for the Whiz Bang 3X, preferring to cover their backsides in case the product doesn't garner the forecasted market share. Gloria needs to find a champion quickly to help her ensure she's got all her bases covered with that delivery system.

If Gloria pulls off the successful launch of the Whiz Bang 3X, she has the real potential of taking over the position of vice president of product development that will be open when Pete retires next year. She's yearned for this opportunity to expand her career for the last five years and has steadily taken on more and more responsibility to become the primary candidate for succession.

Rather than viewing the delivery system discovery as a crisis, Gloria sees the opportunity not only to handle the volume issue but also to preempt the scalability issue the company would face as a fast follow-on when the Whiz Bang 3X is successful. She's hoping her forethought and vision will help to ensure she's selected as the next vice president. She also knows if it doesn't work, she'll likely be looking for a new job because the Whiz Bang 3X is coming to market only months before a competitor's product that claims to answer the same needs in the marketplace.

The rumblings she's hearing from her company's current customers tells her that the Whiz Bang 3X is definitely what they need. And the new compliance regulations under government review will cause added market urgency if they are approved—and that outcome seems likely. In order to move at the speed necessary to meet project timelines, Gloria has to get consensus with a number of influencers fast. She needs a delivery system vendor who can help her gain knowledge quickly, as well as the confidence to step out on the ledge and do the right thing for both her company and its customers.

Can you see how you'd be able to help Gloria if you knew all about her situation and offered a delivery system that would match her goals? Before you think, "yeah, but I'll never get close to knowing Gloria's situation," consider the following possibilities for how you might know enough to get a good handle on this information:

- The need for a product like the Whiz Bang 3X has been discussed on industry blogs, articles about the subject have appeared in industry e-zines, and several analysts have predicted its development by a company like Gloria's.
- The new compliance regulations have been dissected in the business press, so you know that the challenge of addressing the changes they mandate is going to become a high priority for the existing and potential customers Gloria's company serves, as well as companies like hers.
- You're monitoring competing companies that sell delivery systems similar to yours. One company issues a press release listing new customers. You know this company has issues with volume capacity because several of your new customers switched from that company to yours. Gloria's company is on that list of new customers.
- From monitoring your customers and prospects over time, you've seen the decision makers on similar projects ascend to the position of vice president of product development and know that this is a likely career-path choice for someone like Gloria.
- You are a member of a social network that includes companies like Gloria's and see comments and questions that indicate the need for higher volume capacity in delivery systems is increasing.

This type of information is available. The challenge is connecting the dots. However, it's exactly the type of information you need to get started in defining a niche that helps you to create a persona that likely will come very close to addressing Gloria's scenario. Alternatively, input from your salespeople can help you to create a persona similar to Gloria's based on what they've learned during recent wins and longer-term customer relationships.

It's important to remember that personas evolve and change along with their environments. You cannot create a persona and then never revisit it for tuning and tweaking. You must be diligent about monitoring related changes and advances and updating your company's personas as warranted.

Keeping yourself attuned to factors that affect your personas is made easier once you've identified what types of information to track to help you tune relevance. Chasing all available information will just confuse the issue. If the insights you gain from the information aren't actionable, they're not useful. Using Google Alerts, Twitter, and Really Simple Syndication (RSS) feeds can simplify the effort spent on acquiring the information you need to stay in step. Consider setting up Google Alerts for industry terms and keywords your prospects use in relation to the problems your products address. Subscribe to the RSS feeds for blogs and industry portals that address topics relevant to your prospects. Use a widget such as Tweet Grid or Tweet Deck to follow people who could be your prospects to learn what interests them.

This type of niche plus persona combination helps direct your eMarketing strategy to closely align with what your ideal prospects need, what they're concerned about, and how they may make buying decisions. When your content reflects their interests, engagement levels grow, and so does your credibility as a valuable business partner.

## Chapter 4

# Leverage Your Buyer Synopsis

B uyers learn about things they need to know at the time they need to know them. Trying to expose them to information beyond their needs pushes them faster than they may want to go. In this chapter you'll learn how to use a buyer synopsis to create a content-development plan around components that can be combined in different formats and at varying lengths to answer top-of-mind needs.

A *buyer synopsis* is a short-story version of what prospects may experience when they set out to solve a high-priority, complex problem. It marries a specific persona with a problem-to-solution scenario to serve as a guide for high-value content development that delivers the information prospects need throughout the stages of the buying process. A buyer synopsis will simplify and unite the customer-focused story you share at each stage, pulling your buyers forward in their buying process with your company.

## CREATE A BUYER SYNOPSIS

Four steps are involved in creating a buyer synopsis. Once you've created a buyer synopsis, you'll have a guide for each eMarketing program you develop. The synopsis can be reused and refined as you learn more about your prospects with each successive program.

### *Step 1: Select a Problem-to-Solution Scenario for a Specific Persona*

Your buyer synopsis will be focused on one persona in a particular niche that needs to solve a specific priority issue. The first step is to select the persona and match it to one problem. Then complete the "Customer-Focus Tune-up" below. Don't forget to include the influencers you've identified during persona creation because the buyer will need to get consensus from them to make a purchase decision.

---

**CUSTOMER-FOCUS TUNE-UP**

This exercise is designed to help flip your focus away from your company and products to your prospect's perspective and develop content designed to

*( Continued )*

---

engage your prospects incrementally at each stage of the buying process. To do this exercise correctly, you must put yourself into your prospect's shoes. Answering the questions from your company's perspective will not produce the best results.

**Create Customer Focus**

1. Choose and define a problem that you know the selected buyer persona is encountering.
2. Begin by asking yourself and your team what that persona will need to know to think strategically about solving that specific problem. Don't discount any ideas. Put them all on the list.
3. Take each idea on the list and discuss why it's important and to whom it's most important. You may find ideas that relate more to influencers and stake holders than to the specific persona. Move those ideas to a separate list. You'll need them.
4. Once you have a list of ideas your prospects need to know more about, delve deeper and jot some notes for each one about why and how your prospects are affected by that idea in relation to the problem they're trying to solve. Often this discussion will spawn additional ideas you overlooked in the preceding step.

The Customer Focus Tune-up is designed to help you generate an outline for the overarching story of your eMarketing initiative. It will help you gain the insights you need to design content that addresses each stage of the buying journey. People don't always think linearly to reach a complex purchase decision. Each of your prospects may vary in the ways they access and ingest information, but all the questions and concerns they have must be answered before they commit to a purchase decision. If you can address their needs logically, you'll build credibility as a specialist focused on solving their problems in a way that matches how they think about them, enabling you to move prospects farther through the pipeline in less time and produce more qualified sales opportunities.

### Step 2: Determine What that Persona Needs to Know to Buy

Your responsibility as a marketer extends farther in each direction of the buying process than it ever has before. It begins with the status quo, and it continues until the prospect commits to buying and beyond. There are critical knowledge points your prospect must feel confident about to make that final decision. By identifying these points, you can map the components of required knowledge for each buying stage.

### Step 3: Assign What Prospects Need to Know during Various Buying Stages

In the sidebar are critical questions designed to help you think about what your prospects need to know during each stage of their buying journey. Remember to answer them from the persona's viewpoint.

1. *Status quo to priority shift:*
   a. Why should I change?
   b. What will happen if I don't?
   c. What triggers would force me to need to solve this issue?
   d. How is the issue impacting my industry?
   e. How are my peers and competitors addressing the issue?
2. *Research to options:*
   a. What do I need to know to think strategically about solving the problem?
   b. Are there best practices I can refer to?
   c. Who's got the expertise to add the most value to the project?
   d. What are the periphery impacts I need to consider?
   e. What options and alternatives are available?
3. *Step backs to options:*
   a. Which risk probabilities would make me falter?
   b. Whose disagreement could cost me the decision to move forward?
   c. Which stakeholder's objectives might not get addressed by an option?
   d. What if my end users won't adopt the solution?
   e. How will I manage realigning the business processes the solution affects?
4. *Validation to choice:*
   a. Why should I trust your company to help me solve my issue?
   b. Beyond the initial project budget, what's the total cost of ownership?
   c. What's the return on investment, and how long will it take to realize?
   d. What will happen when my needs scale and extend to meet new objectives?
   e. How are people/companies like me/mine finding success with this choice?
   f. In what ways will choosing this solution affect my professional status?

By answering each of these questions, you'll build a picture of the thinking process this persona may experience as she works through the buying process to build a business case. Asking your salespeople to participate in this exercise can help to round out the synopsis. They have valuable insights that marketing doesn't have ready access to. Additionally, involving your frontline customer service and support people can provide answers to several of the questions in stages 3 and 4.

Be open to adding new questions under each stage as they come up in discussions with sales, support, and service people. This list is only a starting point. Building a customer consensus with all the people who play roles in acquiring, retaining, and growing your customer base ultimately will contribute to alignment and consistency across your customer-facing departments.

### Step 4: Map Content to Persona Needs for Each Stage

Use your answers to the questions in Step 3 to help you map relevant content resources to each buying stage. This process will tell you definitively how well your current content is designed to appeal to this persona as she tries to solve the selected problem. It also points to content you'll need to create to fill in the gaps or ways you can modify existing content to answer needs in different stages. Considering that it takes upward of 10 to 12 touches during a complex sale before your prospects feel comfortable enough to ask for sales conversations, being prepared to address what they need at each stage helps them build momentum for their buying process, shortening your time to revenues.

## USE SOCIAL MEDIA FOR PERSONA DEVELOPMENT

Social networking is making inroads in B2B marketing. Several social media options to consider exploring for B2B persona development are LinkedIn, Twitter, and industry-related blogs. Check out industry online magazines that enable readers to submit ratings and comments. Reviewing comments on both industry sites and blogs that focus on topics of interest to your prospects provides insight into audience reactions about the content they're publishing. Those readers could very well be your prospects and customers.

To leverage all that these sites can offer, marketers need to listen more than participate until they've determined how best they can contribute to the conversation without trying to monopolize it. Start by seeking out your customers and prospective customers on social applications and listening to them. By monitoring their conversations, marketers can verify that they're actually creating personas and content that address issues in ways that are relevant to prospects like them.

Blogs are becoming accepted as valuable resources for niche topics. Guy Kawasaki's Alltop.com is a terrific aggregator of blogs grouped by topic. Search for blogs that talk about related industry topics, and look for the ones that have the most comments. Often the comments are more telling than the blog posts. You can learn a lot about how people just like your prospects are thinking about issues that are important to them. By using blogs and the comments on them strategically, you'll have a great validation tool for tuning your buyer synopsis.

As you listen to what's being said, pay attention to the phrases and terminology your prospects—or people like them—use to discuss topics related to the problems your products solve. Gauge the tone of their responses to try to determine the level of urgency they feel about solving the problem. Are they frustrated about a specific aspect of the problem? Do they agree or disagree with the stance the author took in the article or blog post they're commenting on? Perhaps they're offering suggestions for how they think the problem can be handled. The idea is to learn as much as you can from their input and evaluate these insights against your personas and content-development plan.

By using a sampling of topical social networking sites, you'll be better able to validate the assumptions and perspective stance you took while creating your buyer synopsis. The information is timely, enabling you to keep your personas in step with the evolution of your target markets. At the speed of change today, you can't afford not to develop tools that keep you abreast of your prospects' current interests and priorities.

## PERSONALIZATION—ONE STEP AT A TIME

All the tools presented in the Customer Consensus section—customer profile, persona, and buyer synopsis—are designed to help you personalize the way you interact with your prospects and customers. The goal is to create increased engagement levels. When you consider that 37 percent of executives say that 25 to 75 percent of lost sales are directly related to a lack of engagement,[1] the results from personalizing your content can be impressive.

What's important is that you take the first step. Personalization is—and always will be—an iterative process. There's nothing more constant in today's business environment than change. Focus on achieving one objective that brings you closer to your prospects and then layer on another. As you monitor the progress of your eMarketing strategies during execution, you'll find many ways to evolve the tools. Work more closely with personas and buyer synopses to get better at stepping into your prospect's perspective. Every step forward will bring rewards and payoffs. If you falter, make an adjustment and keep going. Personalization is not a perfection process—it's a human undertaking. Get started now. Take one step at a time to get to know your prospects and customers better. The changes you see will be worth the effort.

*Chapter 5*

# The Buying Process

The buying process for a B2B complex sale has shifted in recent years. This shift means that much of the time that was previously spent with salespeople is now spent reviewing online resources. For this reason, it's imperative to be found in the places where your prospects are looking. Now more than ever, your company must be recognized as a source of relevant knowledge that pulls prospects into the sales pipeline. Well-executed content will play a bigger role in building trusted relationships that get salespeople invited into the process more efficiently.

Consider the differences in marketing's reach from traditional outbound ("Past") to interactive marketing ("Now") shown in Figure 5.1. Notice that the handoff from marketing to sales is now much farther into the pipeline. The shift moving sales activities to later in the buying process has created a gap that must be filled, and one way to fill it is through relevant content to keep prospects engaged. Marketers who successfully create extended engagement will progress buyers more quickly to sales readiness.

In the past, marketing created content that focused on making prospects aware of the company's products so they'd consider shifting their buying dollars. Prospects who showed a bit of interest were then placed into the sales process. This approach was successful prior to the

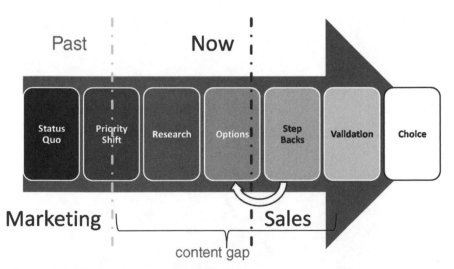

**Figure 5.1** The buying process past and present.

Internet because prospects needed to talk with salespeople to get the information they needed to solve their problems. We all know that this is no longer the case.

Buyers now can scour the Internet, attend Webinars from their offices, and even participate in virtual events without ever speaking directly to a salesperson. Companies who are investing in customer-focused content are capturing the lion's share of prospect attention. Marketing's responsibility expands beyond interest generation to building engagement throughout the buying process. Yes, even after salespeople become involved.

Notice in Figure 5.1 the inclusion of "Step Backs" in the buying journey. They've always been there, but they haven't been specifically recognized as a viable buying stage or content opportunity. Buyers rarely conclude a purchase without revisiting considerations. Most often this is due to ideas that surface throughout their research and options evaluations. Creating content designed to address additional questions and considerations is critical to keeping prospects involved with salespeople and to moving them forward in their buying process.

By coordinating content strategy with sales efforts, marketers can ensure that the company's story is told consistently from status quo through choice. By working collaboratively with marketing, sales-people will spend a lot less time recreating collateral that diverges from the corporate story. They'll spend more face time with buyers working consistently to extend that same story. Salespeople will close more deals because they're in synch with the needs and expectations of potential buyers. Since marketing has communicated throughout every stage of the cycle and in more detail with buyers, aligning with sales to advance relationships based on that foundation reduces costs and shortens time to revenue.

## THE ROLE OF CONTENT IN THE BUYING PROCESS

It's important to remember that every interaction you have with a prospective buyer is an opportunity to demonstrate the experience they'll likely receive as your customer. Marketers who focus on increasing the relevance of their content can make huge strides in building engaged relationships with prospects. The availability of online publishing and distribution options makes interacting with prospects easier than ever.

Vary the type of content you publish, and you can broaden your reach within target markets as you address alternate learning preferences with multiple content types. Additionally, display versatility in your content and you'll demonstrate the versatility of your company. It's subtle, but the impact is not lost on your prospects. In addition, marketers who develop content that addresses the mindset of prospects during specific stages of their buying process connect more readily and more often.

### Map Content to Buying Stage

Prospects search for different information at each stage in their buying process. By defining the interests and needs for each stage, you'll see parallels that enable the repurposing and use of content designed for one stage in another.

**Status Quo**   The prospect is experiencing a limitation, problem, or obstacle with his current situation but hasn't yet chosen to actively address it by buying a solution.

*Content focus:* Introduce the prospect to industry trends that point to developing issues and the business value of adopting change. You also can direct prospects toward educational articles and Webinars about problems and pain points that help them learn they don't need to continue to deal with those limitations and why they shouldn't. Or you can show them how innovations can broaden opportunities and effectively eliminate those limitations. Introduce them to new considerations, and talk to them about what companies like theirs are doing.

**Priority Shift**   The prospect is now actively interested in educating himself about what change might mean for his company. He needs to think about the strategic impact of solving the problem and choose a direction to explore.

*Content focus:* Draw positive attention to yourself during this stage by providing educational content that builds off the problem and pain-point focus used for status quo prospects. Additionally, expand on the industry trends with hard facts and statistical information they can use to shift consensus. Remember to focus on the business value of solving the problem, and use hard data in a story format, not as stand-alone facts without context for the prospect's current situation. Keep your focus on the problem-to-solution scenarios.

**Research** The prospect is committed to resolving the problem and is focused on building a business case. He is looking for leading experts on the subject and the potential outcomes he can realistically plan to accomplish.

*Content focus:* This is the time to put your expertise into play. At this point, prospects have basic knowledge about possible solutions, and they're committed to solving the problem. Discuss risk and how your expertise helps to mitigate it proactively. Expand their thinking to illuminate the overlapping issues that may be offshoots of the project so they can plan to address them. In short, help them to enlarge their thinking in strategic ways. Make sure you consider the needs of project influencers, various stakeholders, and colleagues.

**Identifying Options** The prospect has built a business case, feels confident in the level of competence he has acquired about the subject matter, and is narrowing his focus to possible options for a short list. This is quite often the transition point to a sales opportunity.

*Content focus:* This is the opportune time to showcase customer success stories and demonstrate how your customers have achieved successful project implementations and business value. Discuss industry developments that expose the costs of the problem, and work to confirm your buyer's resolve to remedy the issue. Most important, make sure you focus on exposing the added value your customers get by partnering with you to achieve complex problem resolution—expertise they won't get if they buy a similar product down the street.

**Step Backs** The buyer has identified your company as a viable option, but new information or concerns have introduced hesitation and reevaluation.

*Content focus:* The content leveraged during this stage should engineer a reversal, effectively turning the buyer around and putting him back on track. Pay strict attention to what makes buyers back up. What are the issues they aren't yet comfortable with? The more you learn, the better you can tweak your process to include this reassurance at earlier stages. When you address areas of concern during step backs, the content used needs to be transparent. The more up front your company is and the more individualized your focus on the buyer's concerns, the easier it will be to get things moving forward again—not to mention the escalation of your company's credibility.

**Validation for Beliefs**   The buyer has put your company on his short list and needs to make sure that his assumptions are true before making the final decision.

*Content focus:* This is the time when the viability of your company is reassessed. Make sure the "About Us" company Web page, support-services content, and media sections of your Web site are written with buyers in mind. Freshly updated and relevant results achieved by your existing customers will stand out most to your buyers and are essential to their decision. Testimonials from customers in their own words are also powerful validation tools. Additionally, analyst and research reports that highlight your company are useful.

**Choice and Commitment**   The buyer is ready to make a purchase decision. How you handle the final negotiations, reassure any wavering influencers, and transition them to becoming your customer is the final stage. Marketing can help with this stage by creating a customer-focused proposal template. Remember that the purchase is about the customer. It's best not to lead with six pages of company information. Put your customer front and center.

## APPLY CONTENT TO PERSONAS

When you've addressed all your prospects personally and individually and built a one-to-one relationship with each of them, then you've perfected engagement. As nice as this sounds, realistically, there just aren't enough hours in the day or marketing resources to focus on prospects one at a time. The key is to use personas to guide your content development, getting you much closer to personalization than you would with generalized messaging.

Keep your prospects engaged and get closer to that one-to-one ideal by using marketing automation systems. These systems increase your ability to get the right information out at the right time by structuring drip marketing touches for prospect nurturing. They also enable marketers to monitor responses in real time and gauge interest levels. Automation systems provide nearly instant feedback about your content's ability to accomplish nurturing goals. However, the real beauty of marketing automation is that it provides visibility to individual prospect behavior.

The most important thing about applying personas to your nurturing content is simply to get started. Begin with one buyer synopsis, and expand as you learn with each successive campaign. If you need to keep your current eMarketing moving while you create that synopsis, then choose a job role within one industry and start with that as the first iteration.

Content topics are ripe for expansion and repurposing to meet the needs of different buying stages. Figure 5.2 demonstrates one way to get multiple uses from a well-researched topic. When you develop an

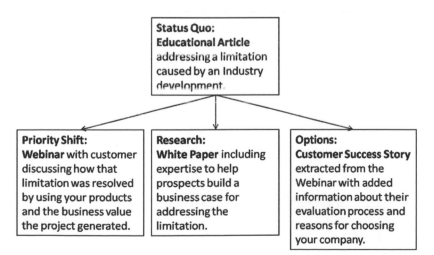

**Figure 5.2** One topic → multiple content resources.

eMarketing strategy, you've created a plan to make the best use of your available content-development resources to meet the needs of your prospects. When you're charged to do more with less, reducing the resources needed to generate continuous engagement and help you create a consistent storyline pays off.

In Figure 5.2, the same topic is used to create four content resources to meet prospect needs during different buying stages. An eMarketing strategy streamlines content research-and-development efforts. All four pieces are focused on the same problem-to-solution scenario. Each builds on another resource to continue enlarging the story. This consistent story delivery builds higher levels of engagement.

Once the prospect has read one piece, the rest of the story ties into background information your prospect is familiar with, easing the effort of assimilating the new information. Because the story becomes more familiar with additional exposure, prospects stay engaged to learn more and begin anticipating the results enjoyed by your customers.

## PART III

# NATURAL NURTURING

Persona-driven engagement accelerates and expands revenue opportunities.

## Chapter 6

# Put the Natural in Nurturing

Instead of your company chasing prospects, you want your prospects to find you when they need you. Becoming ubiquitous in your market space is one of the critical components of attraction marketing. Natural nurturing puts your company in front of prospects wherever they are—it doesn't depend on them already existing in your database. Your content needs to address the issues that drive people to need your products. It also should be mapped to each stage of the buying journey and tell an engaging, consistent story that initiates dialogue. Finally, you need a framework to pull it all together for execution, with a good degree of transparency and authenticity mixed in to increase credibility. When natural nurturing is done well, seeking out your company to help solve a pressing problem will seem like the most obvious response in the world to your prospective customers.

A recent study by IDG Market Fusion discovered that buyers find relevant content that meets their needs only 42 percent of the time. In fact, this lack of relevant content affected a vendor's overall chance of being included as an option for a buyer's consideration by 45 percent.[1] An optimal eMarketing strategy provides for the ongoing presentation of customer-focused problem-to-solution scenarios that naturally attract prospects to your company's solutions. Your prospects' engagement is strengthened as they increasingly "see" themselves in the story you're sharing. They become involved as active participants who can visualize how your company will improve their future with a successful project outcome.

Natural nurturing goes beyond staying in touch with a prospect database. The objective is to stimulate thinking that engages potential buyers and expands your reach. Natural nurturing is also about sharing your expertise through real-world scenarios that prospects quickly understand and appreciate. For nurturing to be successful, the story you're sharing needs to evolve along with your prospects' interests and concerns as they work to address high-priority issues.

It's time to shift your thinking. Think of today's marketing department as a publisher with a variety of content channels at its fingertips that can provide you with a larger communications reach than you've ever had before. Even though 80 percent of companies say that they "found" their vendors rather than their vendors finding them,[2] chances are high that their initial discovery was somewhere other than your corporate Web site.

The best defense is a proactive offense. Companies who embrace the diversity of media sources that B2B prospects use are seeing lucrative results. Available media sources include blogs, industry e-zines, LinkedIn profiles and groups, and aggregator sites such as Digg, Technorati, Insight24, SlideShare, and YouTube. It may sound counterintuitive, but search engines also have taken on social status. Their very nature of returning the most relevant matches to phrases used in search queries has made them the go-to resource when seeking information. With content developed to meet customer needs that match their perspectives, your company will be found when prospects go looking.

Many B2B companies are just beginning to use some of these techniques. The key to taking your marketing stories social is to make sure the story you share on one channel is consistent with the stories your prospects will see on other channels. Hooking all the different media together to create a story flow can help you take your nurturing way beyond drip marketing campaigns that rely on e-mail communications. While marketing automation connects only identified prospects with your story, taking your story social helps to attract a wider audience of prospects to discover and engage with your company's expertise.

Delivery of content is not the issue. It's the creation of relevant content. The traditional approach of one-size-fits-all content is the basis of ineffective nurturing. Marketers need to embrace content development and make sure that content is available through the online channels your prospects use.

Two elements can make your eMarketing strategies shine. The first is to use your content to create a conversational context to attract inbound interactions. The second is to leverage those interactions intelligently.

## CREATE A CONVERSATIONAL CONTEXT

Buyers search the Internet with increasing frequency. They're looking for fresh content that provides insights geared toward answering their questions and addressing their problems in ways that apply to their specific situations. Marketers, however, tend to provide company-focused content that's published based on their organizations' agendas for new products, features, and innovations. This content has no context for your prospects. Nor is it usually conversational.

One of the best ways for marketers to grasp what's meant by *conversational context* is for them to study popular blogs. Business blogging has hit the mainstream. Blogs are rated in the top four types of content that buyers find valuable during their status-quo and research stages of the buying process.[3] Articles are number one. Blogs are usually focused on sharing information, insights, and opinions about a particular topic or subject-matter area the blogger is passionate about. Businesses are actively leveraging blogs to create thought leadership and humanize their companies through interactive dialogue. Some do this better than others. By studying them and learning to write in a way that invites dialogue, marketers can add some humanity to their marketing. You can show your prospects that there are people behind the logo. And this goes a long way in an increasingly "social" online environment.

Complex sales topics are discussed in a growing number of blogs, and are considered instrumental sources in helping their audiences learn about relevant issues. Readers post comments and ask questions to learn more, engaging in a virtual dialogue that can help you learn more about their perspectives. A conversational blog can add credence to the information available on your corporate Web site, as well as gauge topic relevancy and interest from your audience. Your business blog can help promote registration for Webinars; provide downloads of e-books, articles, and white papers; and invite prospects to schedule personal appointments.

Exposing the human side of your company is becoming a requirement for those who want to increase engagement with their customers. Blogging enables company experts to share their knowledge and thoughts in a less formal and more open manner than on their corporate Web sites. A great way to use a B2B company blog is to write commentary and share expertise about the impact your company has on helping customers solve problems. Your intention is to become a valued resource for information on that subject. Don't mention your product names or talk about your company. Instead, stay clearly focused on the issues that interest your audience.

The beauty of a blog post is that it can be as short as a few sentences with a link to another resource, or your post can run as long as you need to do justice to your subject. You can include graphics, embed videos, share slide decks, reference other online resources, and expand the coverage of a topic by tackling it from a variety of angles. Blog posts can increase your content flow, spreading your ideas to a much wider audience than you'd otherwise have access to. Not only can your blog help your company get "found" through better search-engine results, but those results also can be augmented and spread further when other bloggers who talk about the same subjects link to you, naturally expanding your reach into new audiences.

An effective B2B company blog requires the commitment of both time and strategy. Keeping your audience interested and your blog relevant demands taking the time not only to post consistently but also to listen to the community your audience listens to and partic ipates with. Your posts also should be tied in with the stories your marketing programs are sharing. If they're not, you'll only create a dissonance with prospects who receive your e-mails, visit your Web site, and read your blog. Consistency is critical. Every content expo-sure your company gains online can help you build engagement with potential customers. The benefits of listening to the community and monitoring the participation on your blog can add healthy input to your eMarketing strategy.

For your blog to gain traction, it's important to include links to others, making it possible for you to gain links back in return. Your company doesn't know everything, so don't act like your blog lives in a vacuum. Instead, embrace other thought leaders, and link back to their content if you think your audience will benefit from the expo-sure. Be generous and become a trusted source by adding additional insights that extend the value of the blog post or article you reference. This is what causes others to pick up links to your posts. A conversa-tional context lies in the addition of valuable ideas that provoke new responses to the original article.

When you consistently provide valuable content, you'll find your blog posts referenced by a variety of sources over time. Your posts may become syndicated on an aggregate community blog—such as Alltop—or may be added to Digg or Delicious by your avid readers. Include a blogroll of like-minded blogs or blogs that discuss related subjects your readers will be interested in learning more about. If you're concerned about providing links to other content beyond your own, let it go. With blogging, you get as much in return as you give. Remember, the primary concern of a business blog should be to deliver the highest value possible to your audience. This is definitely a "do unto others as you would have them do unto you" undertaking.

Controlling the conversation is no longer your domain. Shaping the conversation with your expertise, insights, and commentary, however, is the key to creating interactive dialogue. Influence is a payoff for those who blog selflessly and stay in tune with their audience's interests. Don't forget to visit and comment on your customers' blogs. Their peers are likely reading, and well, don't you want more customers like them?

Finally, don't be afraid of a little controversy. Controversial subjects arouse passion in your audience and generate community conversations. Choose your topics wisely, and take a stand your company believes in. Invite discussion. Be human. If someone posts a negative comment, think carefully about how you answer. Being defensive is not the right approach. Instead, focus on finding something positive to say that can reshape the conversation.

## THE ROLE OF RICH MEDIA

Interactive media opportunities are taking center stage across much of the Internet. Blogs are only one option that can be used to attract prospects to a variety of rich content, which, when made available in wider variety of formats and locations, will attract prospects to your company. Incorporating rich media into marketing story programs increases your reach and exposure to existing and new audiences.

When people see ideas in different contexts, they have a higher propensity to learn through subtle repetition. Keep in mind that different content types can be used to present ideas in different ways. And since it usually takes seeing the idea three times before it sticks with your prospects, consider including multiple formats based on the same information to help build your story.

### Video

YouTube is the standard for putting videos into public circulation. The benefit of YouTube is that it also enables you to easily embed the video on your blogs and Web sites. To create traction with a complex sale, entertainment must be tempered with relevant information. The trick is in creating a video with substantive content provided in an engaging way. The "talking head" monologue generally is not engaging, although an interview format works well if the subject is focused on issues important to your prospects and customers.

Focus on providing value. When you apply a video to your storyline, consider how it plays with other content. A video should be used to complement and extend the story you're already sharing. Embed it in a blog post, showcase it on a Web page with other related content story pieces, and feature it in your e-mail communications and e-newsletters. When a video is created as part of a consistent storyline, it can be used in a variety of ways to produce a higher interaction stream.

Depending on the use and audience for your video, several minutes is probably long enough. People speak approximately 250 words per minute. The tighter you're focused on your subject, the better use you'll make of 500 to 750 words  and the higher your audience engagement will be. Use the video to expand on an important outcome or issue. Using video as a targeted complement to your eMarketing content can help to emphasize the story you're telling.

### Widgets

*Widgets* are interactive tools that help the user do or learn something. From a B2B perspective, these can be such things as return-on-investment (ROI) and total cost of ownership (TCO) calculators, comparison tools, or perhaps an embeddable Really Simple Syndication (RSS) feed for industry news with your brand as sponsor.

The key is to make sure the widgets have solid pass-along peer value.

In relation to a B2B complex sale, the widget needs to deliver an outcome your prospects and customers will find valuable. By all means include interactive widgets on your corporate Web sites, your blog, and your expertise microsites. Make sure they deliver a valuable insight that helps your prospects to progress in their buying process.

For example, you might provide a widget that allows prospects to enter parameters about their problem and suggests steps they can take or related content they'll find useful, perhaps including independent expertise sources. Another idea is to create informational widgets for different stakeholders in the project that help them answer questions based on their roles. A fun game is one thing, but if it doesn't provide something valuable in the end, it will sustain only momentary attention. And that defeats the point in a considered sale.

### Presentations

When you create presentations, you have a number of tools at your disposal to share what you've presented, expand the lifetime value of the material, and expose new audiences to it. The key consideration is to ensure the story your presentation tells fits with your eMarketing campaign as a story extension. Try to limit the text on each slide so that every word is necessary and compelling. Tell the story visually with graphics that make ideas easy to grasp. Once you've told your story, a slide deck can be uploaded to slideshare.net and shared with the public. You also can share these presentations on LinkedIn and embed them in your blog, as can your fans. Site users who view your slideshow are invited to post comments about your presentation, favorite it, and share it with their networks, increasing your potential for attracting new audiences.

### Webinars

Webinars can make for wonderful content that both nurtures and generates demand, provided that they're focused on the issues that interest your prospects and are not solely a demo of your solution. Expand the reach of the content you've already created by posting archived versions on your Web site and microsites so they can be found in multiple places and syndicating them on a Web site such as Insight24.com. Syndication Web sites invite users to rate, share, tag, and enter comments about the Webinar, as well as giving them the option to e-mail it to their peers and colleagues. How much more responsive do you think the influencers and stakeholders in a project would be if they receive a recommendation to watch your Webinar from a colleague rather than via an e-mail sent by your company?

Video, widgets, presentations, and Webinars present a variety of formats for content development and distribution. With natural nurturing, the point is to increase the flow of information related to your marketing story and attract interest. Posting rich media online and making it available from other locations beyond your Web site provides the opportunity to attract more traffic, build greater awareness, and demonstrate the value your company can add. Tackling your subject from differing angles in each format provides the repetition needed to get an idea to take hold.

The more places your company is seen online, the more credible your company becomes. Although your corporate Web sites and microsites are critical components of an eMarketing strategy, participating beyond the domains you control aids in your ability to generate interactive dialogue with potential and existing customers.

## LEVERAGE INBOUND INTERACTIONS

As you begin marketing interactively, you'll be inviting users to participate via comments, feedback, ratings, referrals, and reviews. Your audience may tweet about you, blog about your content or company behavior, and participate in e-mail exchanges in response to your nurturing campaigns.

Whether your company gets involved in actively creating online interactions, or people choose to post about you on their own, you need to consider the value of each impression. Most companies respond and move on or don't respond at all. To optimize natural nurturing results, it's important to consider how to best embrace the participation your eMarketing generates. Consider how what you learn and experience about your prospects can be used to enhance your eMarketing strategy. The relationships and loyalty you build will progress your prospects toward purchase.

According to research into social technographics, more people are spectators than creators and critics combined.[4] Someone motivated to actually respond to your content and your company, whether positive or negative, is providing valuable input you can use.

Negative feedback can be turned into a positive experience based on your response. Consider a negative response to be an invitation to interact, just as you would a positive one. People like to be recognized for their opinions, insights, and thoughts. Soliciting further feedback can teach you about the impact of something you've done, the reaction to a stance you've taken on an issue, or the response to a self-focus you were unaware would have ramifications within your community. Be grateful that you've been made aware of the issue. Address it graciously, and thank the user who thought it worthwhile enough to participate.

A positive response can be an indication that the topic you selected was indeed of high interest to that person and perhaps to more people like them. Do you have that segment or persona type on your radar? What else can you learn from that person to help you make an even better connection with people who have similar mindsets and needs?

The thing to remember about people who comment on blogs, industry forums, and in response to e-zine articles is that they're likely to do it again. They're also likely to participate within a variety of media channels. How you treat them will play an influential role in determining how they interact with you in the future. In this age of participation, they also may have a following of their own that includes your prospects. Learning can happen even when you're only engaging with a microcosm of a prospect segment.

But don't go changing everything because of one person's response. Do make sure that you complete a positive interaction with the person, and put the insights you've gleaned on your radar to test their validity. If you feel strongly about it, test the waters and see if shifting your stance slightly in relation to that feedback will create increased dialogue with your prospects. Sometimes it's the little shifts that make the biggest differences.

Consider how you can include what you learn by paying tribute to interactive exchanges. This may be accomplished by including a reference to a comment in a blog post or even inviting that person to share her story about the difference working with your company has made. Shared stories can make great videos as well. The point is that getting people to respond is hard. Getting them to respond when there's no payoff is even more difficult. Remember, natural nurturing means that interactions, content, and experiences will have a consistency and relevance your prospects will learn to count on and anticipate. Learn from them at every opportunity, and your nurturing campaigns will garner more reach and sales readiness than ever.

## Chapter 7

# Capitalize on Cause

In a complex sale, *cause* is whatever compels a prospect to actively seek resolution for a problem that your company's product addresses. Cause can also be a triggering event, although cause exists farther back in the buying process—often accounting for the underlying imperatives that compel your prospects to take action.

For example, a triggering event could be the discovery that a business system won't scale as needed. The company could decide to do the work to extend the system it has, buy a new system, outsource the capabilities delivered by the existing system, or take a wait-and-see attitude and do nothing at all. When you consider all the possibilities of how prospects can choose to solve their problems, you have the opportunity to create content that addresses each one. You guide prospects to engage your company because your expertise makes your company their best choice. However, if you've only considered one possible reason for your prospects' action, and that's not the way they're thinking, you'll have a much harder time attracting their attention.

By capitalizing on cause, marketers choose to create a content track that addresses a number of possible motives, multiplying their opportunities to catch prospect attention. By addressing different motives, you can learn a lot about your prospects by how they respond. You can continually hone and tweak your nurturing program to connect naturally during your prospects' buying process if you know what motivates them.

Cause requires marketers to apply customer perspective in order to break through the noise around the topic and differentiate their company from competitors. Your prospect's attention can be caught and then shifted subtly by the way you expose strategic expertise during nurturing experiences. A focus on eliciting positive responses can drive buying behavior today and in the future.

To use cause effectively in your eMarketing strategy, you need to be very familiar with how your prospects move through the buying process. Your chances of not only catching but keeping their attention improves if you're also their "anchor" on the subject. If your content has made a lasting and valuable impression, others will have to work harder to unseat your expertise to get through. By incorporating cause with your nurturing programs, getting prospects to take the next step is a natural outcome.

## FROM STATUS QUO TO PRIORITY SHIFT

Status quo is the prospect's current situation. Status quo is comfortable because it's a known entity—even if it's obsolete enough to cause added stress via workarounds and obstacles to desired success. In fact, it's amazing how much companies will endure to avoid change. Change is hard. There are unknown risks, and the path to change often looks murky and raises new questions, problems, and suspicions. Change is perceived as risky—from both a company perspective and that of the individuals on the buying committee.

To fully embrace cause in marketing, marketers must get to know their prospects' status-quo situations inside and out. If you've done the "Customer-Focus Tune-up" exercise in Chapter 4 and worked on creating your buyer synopsis, you're already on your way to understanding the realities of your potential buyers. When you know their status quo, you'll begin to visualize different scenarios that can become sources of cause. Using these scenarios can produce real shifts in the way your company is perceived by buyers.

As your cause expertise develops, you'll begin to see a triggering event before it actually happens. You'll be so attuned to your market that the circumstances affecting it become catalysts for your eMarketing strategies. Gaining this insight is critical. Marketing for a B2B complex sale needs to begin when buyers are sitting in status quo. The problem with marketing to status-quo companies is that the issues you see coming aren't high on their radar yet. However, if you can speak to their existing situation, providing actionable tips and insights about industry trends, you'll create the opportunity to become the prospect's anchor on the subject. You pass the urgency test for relevance because you're speaking to them about their current situation. Consider the difference in engagement potential if you've already helped a company make its current situation better and set it up for a coming change that it will have to address. This proactive marketing approach is what's needed for your company to be top-of-mind before the prospect shifts into buying mode.

### *An Example of How to Impact the Status Quo*

Let's say that a subset of your prospects are currently customers of a competitor. You've heard grumblings about dissatisfaction with a particular element of that competitor's product. Instead of pitching these prospects to switch to your product, provide content that explains how they might work around the issue. Talk about the business value of correcting the problem. Your content is helpful to them because it presents actions they can take now to improve their existing situation. Provide conversational nuggets they can use to begin shifting company consensus toward the change required to deliver needed business outcomes.

When a triggering event happens that makes living with their current situation untenable, you're positioned as the expert resource your prospects will turn to for advice and insight. The story you tell them in status quo should educate them about the business value they can gain, including other successful outcomes your product and expertise can help them to acquire. This does not mean mentioning your products or giving them a sales pitch. It means unveiling possibilities one step at a time—enough to entice them to continue to engage with your content because it's relevant to their situation and offers fresh ideas and strategic solutions.

## BECOME THE ANCHOR

Until your prospects steadily focus on resolving a particular problem, they have no preconceived attachment to a solution. Once the issue is on their radar—even peripherally—they'll start becoming attached to ideas related to that issue's resolution. You want to be the first reference they have to relevant and valuable ideas that apply expertise to the issue at hand. This is why addressing long-term prospects while they're in status quo is effective. This does not mean that you have to be the first company to talk about the problem. What you need to be is the most relevant resource accessed during the time period when prospect attention shifts and the problem in question makes its way onto their radar. If you're already there prior to their shift in thinking, you have an advantage.

When you use a buyer synopsis as a guide for your eMarketing strategy, your content is tuned in to your prospects. This level of relevance is what it takes to become an anchor. General messaging is more about the company than your prospects. It usually includes such things as Webinar invitations, analyst-sponsored white papers, and press releases that lack the cohesiveness of a story. General nurturing content is not designed with the prospect in mind. It's based on your company's agenda.

Design a nurturing program to focus on providing insights and ideas about something relevant to prospective customers, and you will become memorable. Your prospects will naturally begin to anticipate hearing from you. If they use an insight you've provided to them via a nurturing article and see improvements, how much additional mindshare do you think you'll retain versus the competitor who only pushed out its latest product-release information?

Becoming the anchor is also enhanced when your content spurs conversations between your prospects and their influencers and peers. Since prospects most trust someone like themselves, it's becoming an imperative to create and deliver content that inspires people to discuss the ideas you propose.

Generating conversations about your ideas will happen with higher frequency if your content involves influencers. Address each influencer's interests, from her perspective, and your conversations will have more depth and "stickiness." You'll also be facilitating consensus tactics from behind the scenes.

Buying decisions for complex sales increasingly are made by larger groups. Getting a head start by becoming the anchor that stimulates conversations gives you a leg up on the competition.

## KEEP YOUR ASSUMPTIONS ON TRACK

We all know that change is risky, so knowing what's driving a specific need for change is a boon for marketers and salespeople—or it should be. How well you integrate cause into your eMarketing strategy will depend a lot on how on-target your assumptions are about your prospects' concerns. The better you know your prospects, the more on point your assumptions will be. Once prospects see you "get them," they'll interact with you to learn more about how you can help them.

For example, let's assume that a regulatory change has forced your prospects to change the way they process information. You decide that their biggest concern will be the level of difficulty in redefining their information-handling processes. All your communications are focused on "information processing made easy." You're seeing a higher number of prospects rush to engage with you. Why?

Your competitor down the street assumed the big issue for prospects was the retraining issue. The competitior missed the boat, and its prospects have come down the street to your company because you nailed their hot button and are addressing the more relevant concern.

You increased your pipeline volume because before you created communications you leveraged cause. You spoke with existing customers to find out what concerned them about this regulatory issue. You asked them what worried them and what they saw as a beneficial outcome to addressing the issue. You also learned who else in the company the issue is impacting to determine potential influencers. By paying close attention to the words and phrases your customers used, you were able to create more relevant connections. And that attention to detail generated more qualified prospects to interact with your company.

Now you can take this information and create a feedback (Q&A) guide for salespeople involved in these new conversations and ask them to report back with a "face time" read on related concerns heard in meetings, as well as receptivity about solving the issue from the customers and buyers they're speaking with.

Capitalizing on cause often means you need to reassess and not jump to an assumption too fast, just because it seems logical. Since when has addressing problems (buying) been logical? It's a good rule of thumb to consider all the angles, not just the ones that make sense to you. Solving a complex problem almost always will overlap with another situation that must be handled as well. Consider your prospect company's cultural orientation, political obstacles, and interdepartmental relationships and dependencies that could interfere with an agreement to change. Knowing which issue has the highest level of concern will keep your communications focused and relevant. Once you've done this successfully, you'll have a template for how to assimilate cause effectively into your eMarketing strategy.

## CREATE CONTENT THAT PULLS BUYERS FORWARD

B2B marketing for a complex sale is making strides in expanding the volume of demand generation. Leveraging a natural nurturing process that pulls prospects forward along their buying journey will ensure that none of those prospects languishes. A natural nurturing program eliminates the conflict between generating more prospect volume and working toward producing sales-ready opportunities.

Natural nurturing is instrumental in helping you make this transition without sacrificing one side for the other. The focus is on the needs of your potential customers, as well as on helping them self-identify their place in the buying process. When you have valuable content that's highly relevant to your prospects in each buying stage, they actively engage in return, providing you with actionable intelligence. Becoming proficient at reading prospect behavior will help you to initiate interactions that lead to dialogue that helps you move prospects to the next step in buying.

You've all seen those funnel diagrams that show spouts of leads leaking away at different points during the buying process. To plug the leaks and add momentum to your nurturing, you've got to grow engagement. The higher a sense of vested interest your content and interactions creates, the farther and faster your potential customers will move themselves toward becoming sales ready.

Get creative about what you learn about your prospects, as well as how you use that intelligence, and you'll start to shift from a push to an attraction strategy. Monitor online behavior on your Web site, microsites, blog, and in response to your e-mail communications to gauge interests. The more finely focused your content is, and the closer it is mapped to your prospects' buying process, the more you can learn. By noting when a prospect's attention shifts from one topic to another, you can respond accordingly. When you remove barriers and reduce the effort it takes for prospects to access and ingest your content, you increase their satisfaction.

Don't think that once marketing has gotten prospects to identify themselves that you've gotten their devoted attention and can revert to lightweight communications. Engagement can evaporate much faster than you'd think. As prospects spend more time at the edges of the marketing-to-sales process than ever before, your interactions with them are being judged as an example of the experience they'll encounter should they choose to work with your company. They'll move on if your content attempts to focus on your company and products before they're ready to hear about them or if you send them content with lower relevance and less value than they've come to expect.

Instead, focus on increasing their level of commitment with every interaction. With solid commitment in place, the next step of choosing to take action with you is easy and increasingly predictable. And you'll have higher-velocity nurturing that produces more qualified sales opportunities.

### Focus on One Thing

Content that pulls prospects forward does it best when it is focused on one thing. Your prospects' time is squeezed trying to fit in everything that needs to get accomplished, so make it easier for them to engage with you by keeping your messaging and content resources focused.

When you design a nurturing e-mail, you need to know what you want your prospects to do. The favorable possibilities include reply, click the embedded link, and forward to a friend. The unwanted response, but the most reliable one, is delete. Delete happens most often because the content is not of personalized interest, there are too many choices with unclear outcomes, or you're trying to have a sales conversation on your terms.

If you focus on one thing—getting your prospects to click the link, for example—it's easier to create a compelling message. This is because your focus in designing the message is now on what it will take to get that favorable response. If you're concerned about more than one thing, the tendency is to try to do too much. The interpretation by prospects is either that you're focused on what you want or that your company isn't aligned in its communications efforts. Messages that try to do more than one thing result in confusion. A B2B complex sale is not a one-horse race. You won't accomplish the sale with one message.

When you design your e-mail message, make it easy to read or scan with compelling reasons for your prospects to give you the response you've set as your goal. Tell them why they should care and what they'll get. Set an expectation, and then deliver on that promise. When they take the action—let's say clicking through on a link in an e-mail—the content resource you present them with should immediately tie in with the message that brought them there. If you make them stop and focus on a long form, you've changed their focus and have caused them to reevaluate their original choice—to pay you with their attention.

This is why it is so important that you strategically design your nurturing content. If content is designed to match buying stages, linked together in ways that explore depth of interest, and focused on one goal at a time, you'll learn a lot while accelerating their progress. Natural nurturing is about providing the right content at the right time to shape each interaction as a natural progression. Realize that nurturing is an evolving process. Take one step at a time, assess your progress, and keep moving forward.

## Chapter 8

# Construct a Framework for Content Strategy Execution

You've gotten to know your prospects and the problems they're trying to solve, and you've mapped out your content plan. Now it's time to create a framework for how your storyline will flow from your company to the various places your prospects spend their time online. Figure 8.1 shows examples of the components this framework might include, with each one reaching farther out into your prospect community. A healthy level of diversification will improve your eMarketing results by giving your content a presence in the channels used by your prospects.

Disseminating your content across a variety of online channels will help to ensure that a prospect need not exist within your marketing database to be attracted by your natural nurturing programs. Since buyers are not identifying themselves early in the process, you need to proactively position yourself to be found. Research has shown that buyers will search out and read more information by a vendor when the information they are exposed to by that vendor is considered to be valuable and relevant. When content is found to be disappointing, it is because it was not problem-to-solution-focused.[1] These findings emphasize the importance of putting high-quality content into play in a variety of channels to increase demand generation. For example, this is done by connecting related content via hyperlinks, inviting

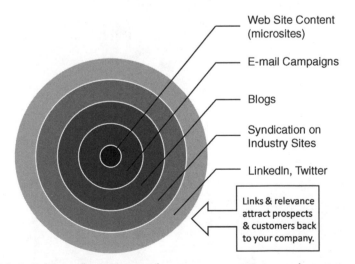

Web Site Content
(microsites)

E-mail Campaigns

Blogs

Syndication on
Industry Sites

LinkedIn, Twitter

Links & relevance
attract prospects
& customers back
to your company.

**Figure 8.1** Content flows outward to engage prospects and customers.

newsletter subscriptions or opt-ins for related information, and distributing educational content via publisher Web sites where buyers often begin their research.

Buyers have ranked search engines as their single most important information source. By optimizing all their content for keyword and longer-tail search results, marketers increase their chances of being found when buyers start looking. But don't overlook the value you can derive from a consistent e-newsletter program. Prospects indicate that e-newsletters frequently influence their decision to actively search for a solution to their problems.

## ASSEMBLE A NATURAL-NURTURING TRACK

The secret to constructing an eMarketing track for a persona is to orient the persona to a problem-to-solution scenario. If you're just beginning to construct nurturing tracks and have no insights into your prospect's interests, consider testing to gauge response levels. Begin with the problem-to-solution scenario that's been most successful for your company. It's likely you have happy customers willing to talk with you, salespeople who know how to sell that product, and a good idea of the urgency level within the industry.

---

### STEPS TO ASSEMBLY

The following steps will help you to create a nurturing track:

1. Select a persona. (If you have a buyer synopsis, skip step 2.)
2. Choose a problem-to-solution scenario.
3. Map related content topics to the buying journey from status quo through choice.
4. Develop the content series from the topics you've mapped.
5. Determine content types, and add those specifics to the map.
6. Select content-delivery options for each content resource in your plan.

---

As you create greater integration, or connectedness, you will increase your exposure and attraction proportionately. Figure 8.2 provides an example of executing a step of your nurturing track.

Execution of the first step in your nurturing track, as shown in Figure 8.2, includes the following actions:

- The status-quo educational article on topic *x* will be posted on the problem-to-solution microsite.
- The corporate Web site will feature a description and link to the microsite article.
- E-mail message number 1 will be sent to the appropriate segmented prospect list with a link back to the article.
- The send will coincide with a blog post on the topic that also includes a link back to the article on the microsite.
- In addition to the article, an offer to opt-in for the related series of content will be featured in a sidebar.
- We'll also post a related question about the topic on LinkedIn with a link back to the article and evaluate answers for extensional blog posts and related articles to expand coverage of the topic and additional exposure for the microsite.

In this example, a microsite serves as the hub for the nurturing track. As you add more content with each step, the resources provide a rich educational environment for your prospects who are interested in resolving the featured issue. The storyline is built with each step,

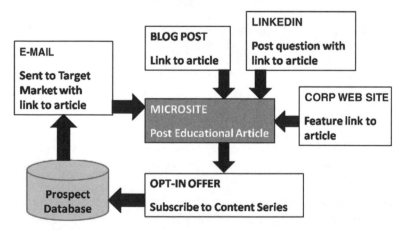

**Figure 8.2** Nurturing steps in execution.

pulling prospects forward in their buying process while building a trusted relationship along the way. Natural nurturing empowers marketers to nurture known prospects and generate new demand at the same time.

## SYNDICATION EXPANDS NURTURING REACH

Drive increased exposure that draws added traffic to your Web properties and results in additional demand generation through syndication. Syndicating your content means enabling it to spread in reach across the Internet. With opt-in being the best method for growing prospect databases, customer-focused content can be put to work externally, helping to attract new audiences.

You've got several options when it comes to syndicating your nurturing content, but the most common is a Really Simple Syndication (RSS) feed. RSS feeds allow subscribers to be notified when new content is published to your blog or even your microsite. Prospects are often more likely to subscribe to an RSS feed than fill out a form because the feed enables them to determine the value of continued engagement without giving away a lot of personal information.

Beyond feeds, there are a number of alternatives for content distribution. Search out industry informational Web sites and online magazines that your prospects frequent. Learn the editorial policies of these sites, and become familiar with the type of content they publish. Publishing sites are always looking for additional content. You'll find your articles published with increasing frequency when you submit content focused on issues that matter to readers.

Association e-newsletters are also a vehicle for content distribution. Learn which newsletters your prospects subscribe to, and sign up to get copies. Note the kinds of articles these newsletters publish, and submit content you've developed that matches in tone and style. Make sure to include a short biography at the end with a link to related information or a microsite that features similar information. Don't use a link that dumps people on your corporate Web site's homepage.

Research agencies often allow companies to submit expertise commentary related to their findings and include it at the ends of their reports. Likewise, industry experts are now publishing e-books addressing specific topics that compile articles written by a number of authors. In fact, your company could be the catalyst. Choose a topic, and invite a selection of industry experts to submit articles for inclusion in an e-book. Select included experts for their audience reach, and invite them to promote their inclusion in the e-book to their followers in addition to your own distribution efforts. Joint distribution can be a great way to discover new audiences that you haven't reached previously.

Syndication can be adapted a bit at a time and prove to be a great extender for the reach of your natural-nurturing programs. The additional opt-ins you generate help to source new business and prove you're in synch with what your market values.

## FREQUENCY, REACH, AND SHIFT

Natural nurturing uses a variety of media channels to share your marketing story. This approach enables you to tell the story a piece at a time with different emphases depending on your audience. The same piece of content can be modified to appeal to the diverse needs of prospects across different segments and buying stages. Increase your attraction value and draw your prospects further into your story with content that is focused on helping them and is interrelated. The higher your attraction value, the more prospects will come to you seeking expertise, putting you in position to connect the dots for them.

When you create story content for a nurturing track, evaluate each piece by asking yourself and your team if you're just creating another touch point or if you're adding a layer of context to the story you're already telling. A layer builds on the story you're already sharing. A touch point may be on the same topic but may not have a natural tie-in with the rest of the story.

Creating a serial "cliffhanger" effect is one way to raise attraction value, provided that you've created material that is interesting, relevant, and valuable to your prospects. Unveil a useful story that keeps your content interesting. Once people know the value of the story, they'll engage with you more often because they're actively interested in learning from you. Your ability to shift their perceptions will grow along with your attraction value.

It's helpful for marketers to remember that prospects are people, not just buyers. With natural nurturing, you don't necessarily need to know the actual identities of your prospects. What you really want is to interest people in your story, your company, and ultimately, your product offerings. Start thinking in terms of attraction value as opposed to simply capturing contact information—you'll find your prospects proactively identifying themselves to you earlier in their buying process.

Here's an example of why natural nurturing is important. Joe Blow may not fit any of the parameters of your target markets, but his respected colleague, Sam Smith, is being nurtured by one of your campaigns. Sam's response is okay, but he's done nothing to indicate a shift in urgency that might signal that he's ready for a sales conversation. That remains true until Joe becomes a trigger when he sees a blog post that references a piece of your story and forwards it to Sam as something he might find useful. You see, Joe knows that Sam is looking to solve a problem your story addresses, so he tries to help him out.

As you continue to monitor Sam's activity via your marketing automation system, you notice that he's now spending more of his attention on your story. Sam proactively visits your Web site to learn more and downloads some of the story pieces he's missed during previous nurturing contacts when he chose not to respond.

## HUBSPOT ATTRACTS CUSTOMERS AT UNPRECEDENTED RATES: A CASE STUDY

Consider the story of HubSpot. While I was writing this book, I began to notice that HubSpot was showing up everywhere. I started following Mike Volpe, its vice president of marketing, on Twitter. I attended a couple of Webinars HubSpot sponsored because the topics and speakers were valuable and relevant to me. HubSpot began sending me e-mail communications with useful articles. As I began to trust that the content provided valuable information, I subscribed to the HubSpot blog's RSS feed. Then I sent Mike a direct tweet and asked him if we could talk. He graciously agreed.

During our conversation, I found pretty much what I'd expected. Mike gave me real-world proof that contagious content approaches deliver significant results to marketing, sales, and the bottom line. Here's proof that natural nurturing works:

- In the last 12 months, HubSpot has grown from 150 to over 1,000 customers.
- Web-site traffic has multiplied by five times in one year.
- Over 80 percent of HubSpot's sales reps are above quota every month. In fact, for each of the three months prior to our conversation, the average sales rep on the team achieved 120 percent of quota.
- HubSpot sales reps do zero cold calling. They're kept busy making follow-up calls in response to qualified inquiries that progress quickly to deals.

So how does Mike cause this outcome? He uses multiple delivery channels to distribute content in a variety of formats. His company has a regular video TV show, hosts Webinars, and has created interactive widgets such as Website Grader, Twitter Grader, and Press Release Grader, that have been used by hundreds of thousands of people to source valuable information. Mike also spends a tremendous amount of time keeping abreast of industry developments and the concerns of prospective customers by monitoring and participating in social media communities such as Twitter and LinkedIn.

Figure 8.3 showcases just a little of HubSpot's natural-nurturing efforts. All of them reference some of the others, making it possible to connect with HubSpot across a number of Web properties. The amount of success HubSpot has achieved is beyond impressive. Who wouldn't love to have their sales reps monopolized with incoming inquiries every single day. Mike has helped HubSpot to achieve this kind of attraction naturally. And he's focused much of his efforts on generating the word of mouth that produces referrals and recommendations, expanding his company's reach and credibility.

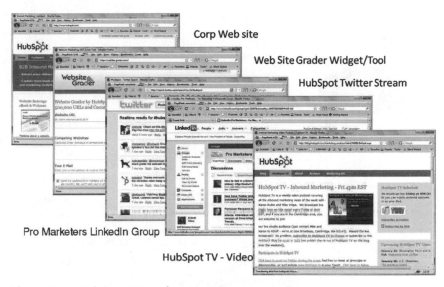

Corp Web site

Web Site Grader Widget/Tool

HubSpot Twitter Stream

Pro Marketers LinkedIn Group

HubSpot TV - Video

**Figure 8.3** HubSpot natural nurturing.

Influencers and recommenders are a critical component of a natural-nurturing philosophy. It's crucial to include them in your eMarketing strategies. After all, peer recommendations and referrals are more influential than most other methods of awareness creation precisely because they're given by people who are respected within their professional communities.

## EFFECTIVE NURTURING EXECUTION

Most companies sell more than one product or solution, each designed individually or as a solution to answer specific customer needs. You'll need more than one nurturing track—one for each of your target markets and the personas within them. The stories you're sharing for each track all need to work together to strengthen your company's overall expertise story as it relates to the problem-to-solution scenarios you address.

Your prospects likely will overlap in the places they frequent online. Make sure that your stories overlap and build on each other. Complementary stories will increase the cumulative results of your natural nurturing.

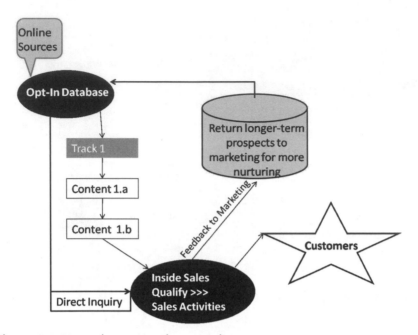

**Figure 8.4** Natural nurturing framework.

Begin by mapping together your nurturing track for one persona and target market. Figure 8.4 is an example of an integrated natural nurturing framework. In this example, you have online sources of content that attract prospects, feeding them into your opt-in database at the top of the diagram. You've constructed one nurturing track based on a problem-to-solution scenario for a target segment and persona. As you commence sending your nurturing communications, attracting prospects to interact with your content, your marketing automation system will score their activities accordingly.

Once a prospect has reached the appropriate level, inside sales follows up with a personal call to learn their qualification level. If the prospect is sales-ready, she is transitioned to a sales rep. If she's not ready, she remains in the nurturing track. As you add nurturing tracks, your inside sales rep can subtly probe to learn whether the prospect's interests are being met or would be better served by moving her to another track.

With an eMarketing strategy, every nurturing communication is planned as an extension of the story you're sharing in relation to a problem-to-solution scenario. Each content resource builds on the last piece and increases the value provided to your prospects. As their engagement with your company grows, interactions will increase. Marketing automation is the system that pulls all your known prospect activity together to give you higher visibility into their virtual behavior. The system provides real-time feedback about the response level of your target segment, enabling you to adjust and tune your content for higher relevance with each step. Marketers are able to respond to prospects in near real time using digital dialogues to encourage exchanges that provide rewards for prospects—and for your company. You have increased capabilities to gather more intelligence to help you know precisely when prospects are ready for sales activities.

Because marketing has taken charge of propelling prospects farther through their buying process, salespeople are selling to more qualified buyers. This means shorter time to revenue and optimized results from your sales force.

## REMEMBER YOUR EXISTING CUSTOMERS

While most nurturing programs are focused on attracting new business, creating nurturing tracks for customers is an important inclusion in your marketing mix for retention and creating up-sell or cross-sell opportunities. Some prospect content may be valuable to existing customers, but it's wise to create content specifically for them. And once you've developed personalized customer tracks, every new customer can be assigned to the one that is right for him. Continuing to build engagement beyond the sale ensures that your customers develop higher satisfaction and loyalty rates.

Once your customers are using your products, determine which triggering events can enable you to extend the value you're providing to them. Using the same technique of personas plus problem-to-solution scenarios, develop content to nurture them toward buying more to gain increasing business value. When you're considered a trusted advisor, it's important to continue offering expertise and education for the next issues they'll face as their situations evolve. It's likely that the elimination of one problem introduces new opportunities customers are now prepared to embrace.

The first year with a customer is important for retention quality and assurance of the continued use of your products because the customer gets the outcomes he needs. Implementation is only the first step. Many companies use only the features of a solution that are required to solve their initial problem. Create a content storyline that helps them to take advantage of every beneficial outcome your products make possible. When your company continues to contribute education and expertise your customers value, they'll have no need to turn to another vendor when new issues surface.

## PART IV

# CONTAGIOUS CONTENT

The right content makes all the difference.

## Chapter 9

# Why Contagious Content Increases Engagement

When a prospect asks the question, "What do you sell?" the question they're really asking is, "What value do you provide that will help me solve a problem or get first-mover advantage?" The reality most B2B companies face is that they know their products, services, and solutions much more intimately than they tend to know their prospects and customers. This is natural. Marketers work with their company's products every day. After all, your company is focused on staying ahead of the competition, comparing your efforts, products, and successes against theirs.

When it comes time to create content, all that knowledge is top-of-mind. It's very clear to you why your product is the no-brainer choice. Your company's value proposition makes perfect sense to you. But your prospects' perspectives are different. They don't have the same investment or interest in your company and products. They care about their goals and the high-value outcomes they can achieve.

Prospective and existing customers also have individualized hot buttons and differing priorities based on their unique circumstances. Some people respond better to the positive spin about how much better life will be with your product or service. Others will relate to a residual benefit that comes about when their challenge is solved in a particular way and take the initiative to get that outcome. Personas and buyer synopses will help you determine how to engage them. Without those tools to guide you, creating content that helps to generate business value is difficult at best.

Back in 2007, David Meerman Scott wrote the "Gobbledygook Manifesto,"[1] and his words, unfortunately, still hold true. David wrote: "Marketers don't understand buyers, the problems buyers face, or how their product helps solve these problems. That's where the gobbledygook happens." Essentially what he says is that this lack of understanding leads marketers to use jargon and terminology designed to mask this deficit. But all that does is confuse your buyers. Even worse, it doesn't help to differentiate your company. David offers this litmus test for verifying if you're guilty of relying on gobbledygook in your marketing: "Take the language that the marketers at your company dreamed up and substitute the name of a competitor and the competitor's product for your own." If the language still makes sense to you, you've got a content problem.

*Contagious content* gains the attention of the prospects you know about and helps your ideas spread to others who haven't yet raised their hands and identified themselves. Content designed for natural nurturing is different from the norm. It differentiates your company because it's clearly focused on your prospects' priorities and perspectives to quickly promote their recognition of value.

Content that is contagious speaks directly to your target markets—engaging prospects as if it were written just for them. It engages primarily because it helps them to visualize their own successful outcomes. According to CSO Insights, 83.7 percent of 1,250 companies surveyed say they see customer expectations increasing.[2] Contagious content helps you keep in step with their expectations. You'll capture their interest because you're discussing solutions to their problems and offering insights and knowledge they need.

Product information does play a definitive role in the buying process. It helps your prospects to do more than verify facts against the beliefs and requirements they've defined. But let's be clear: Product content is compelling in the later stages of the buying process—after your prospects likely have chosen a course of action. It does not create the interest or progression in their buying process that readies them to buy from you. For that, you need contagious content.

Contagious content is effective because it breaks through the noise of relentless information overload we all experience every day. People are exposed to over 5,000 marketing messages from the time they wake up each morning until the time they close their eyes at night.[3] Attracting more than momentary attention is tougher than ever. Contagious content eases that challenge.

## RELEVANCE IS KING

You're probably all familiar with the adage, "Content is king." In today's information-saturated environment, it's more likely that *relevance* is king. If your content doesn't motivate your audience to engage—and perhaps share those ideas with others—it's not doing its job. The only way content can be king is if it's relevant to the people who read it.

Within milliseconds of receiving a message, a prospect intuitively determines whether it's relevant or not. Messages that connect with information your prospects are familiar with and yield conclusions that matter to them are interpreted as relevant. To be relevant, your message must make a worthwhile difference in how a prospect views an existing situation.

Relevance is not an all-or-nothing gambit but more a matter of degree. Your message needs to be more relevant than any other message available to the prospect at the time for it to do more than catch momentary attention. The more worthwhile the degree of relevance your prospects assign to your messaging, the higher will be their level of potential engagement.

This doesn't mean that you should pile on more information in the hope of covering all your bases. The interesting thing about relevance is that it also depends on the amount of effort the prospect must expend in comparison to accessing and understanding other similar messages. This is why the titles and descriptions in search returns, the way you communicate via e-mail, and the style and format of the content itself need to be considered through the eyes of your prospects.

According to Wilson and Sperber, "Relevance theory claims that humans do have an automatic tendency to maximize relevance, not because we have a choice in the matter—we rarely do—but because of the way our cognitive systems have evolved."[4] We look for messages that relate to our memory of similar information. This is why nurturing programs employing contagious content are effective—because they're focused on building an ongoing story. Each cumulative impression adds to the last. You'll find your prospects paying increasing attention as you nurture them, learn more about them, and evolve the relevancy of your content. This is so because it's easier and more efficient for your prospects to expand their information through a resource that's already been validated over time—you and your company.

## SIMPLICITY TRUMPS VOLUME

Word count does not determine value. People tend to remember things in groups of three. If you try to push your marketing content to cover more than three points in relation to your topic, it's difficult to get the retention you need to build ongoing engagement. If the insights your content provides aren't remembered, it isn't perceived as valuable.

The exception to this is content pieces that set expectations for a known quantity, such as "Top 10 Ways to…" or "7 Tips to Increase Your …." However, unless the content provides enough value for your prospects to print it and refer to it, they'll probably only retain the top three items with the most relevance for them. The benefit of the list approach is that you have more chances to hit on three points that connect with them.

Simplicity also means that your content needs to be clear and concise. Scanning has become the reading method of the day. With so much information coming at us from all directions, there's just no other way to keep up. Big words, jargon, and convoluted sentence structures make it more difficult for your prospects to scan and get a quick take on relevance. Without a simple and relevant premise to catch the attention of your prospects, it's unlikely they'll take the time to read your content more thoroughly.

The following e-mail copy produced a 46 percent open rate and a 12 percent click-through for DealerOn, a Web-site solutions provider for the retail automotive industry. The norm for that industry is an 8 percent open rate with a click-through rate of 5 percent.

> Driving online conversions that actually move metal is a bit of an art form. If you're just focused on increasing traffic to your Web properties, your conversions could be taking an unnecessary hit. This article provides 5 tips for optimizing your online efforts to get conversions who purchase vehicles.

The copy is direct to the point the company's prospects were concerned about, it's written conversationally, and the call to action tells them what they'd get when they clicked.

Here are some tips that will help you meet the simplicity challenge:

- *Get your key value statement—your hook—right up front* Set up the problem or issue quickly, and indicate what your prospects will gain by continuing to read. Two to four sentences tops. In the e-mail above, getting online conversions that buy is the hook.

- *Choose words and phrases that mean something to your intended audience* Note the use of *move metal* instead of *sell cars* to match how the prospects in the industry actually talk about that goal.
- *Keep sentences to 30 words or less, varying the length to establish rhythm* The longest sentence in the e-mail copy is 19 words.
- *Involve your prospects by using* you *instead of* we *or* our. We referred to the prospect four times.
- *Read the piece out loud, and edit for clarity.*
- *Remove any filler* Every sentence should add needed information—from your prospect's perspective.

There's a fine distinction between an article that is too short to do the topic justice and one too long to hold attention. Just as you wouldn't tackle a topic such as world peace in a 450-word article, you also wouldn't spend 1,000 words telling people why it's beneficial to tie their shoes.

### CONTAGIOUS CONTENT REQUIRES PLANNING

Contagious content puts an end to the one-off marketing communications that were the norm in the past. A series of disjointed communications because the company is launching a new product, hosting a Webinar, or developing a white paper—all on unrelated topics—is not a recipe for engagement. Marketers focused on presenting high-value, compelling information with each and every story develop contagious content.

The Internet empowers buyers to find and access content. Four of five buyers search the Internet weekly for information about how to solve problems and deal with their high-priority issues.[5] Unfortunately, most marketers only update their content quarterly—and usually in line with a shift in their marketing strategy or another internal reason. In fact, recent research from IDG found that information technology buyers find relevant content only 42 percent of the time.[6] Marketers focused on natural nurturing and contagious content will recognize this as a tremendous opportunity to improve their nurturing results.

Contagious content differentiates you from the competition. You've already spent budget dollars on a marketing automation system to improve communication processes with your prospects. Now take the next step and develop a customer-focused content-development plan. Content development is seen as an overwhelming task that takes too much time, effort, and money from an already stretched-thin budget and overworked marketing staff. The reality is that a well-structured content-development plan can supercharge marketing and sales results. For example, an IT management software company has achieved a 375 percent increase in prospect-to-sales-opportunity conversions in just eight months.

A well-designed, integrated content strategy will give you more content with less effort. You've seen that the right foundation content can be repurposed and reused across marketing segments. Once your prospects discover you provide a stream of consistent and fresh content, revisiting it will become a habit. They will make increased visits to your Web site, blog, and microsites of their own volition, again and again. When prospects come to rely on your company as a valued source of information, you're effectively shaping the way they're thinking about solving their problems—and more inclined to choose your company to help them.

---

### 10 CONTAGIOUS-CONTENT ASSESSMENT TIPS

The following questions will help you to evaluate your existing and new content to ensure that relevance is king.

1. Is the problem, opportunity, or challenge addressed relevant to the selected persona?
2. Is this content resource being deployed at the right buyer stage? For example, if this is the first time you've contacted this person about this issue and your content presumes prior understanding or knowledge, what makes you think the person has it?
3. On a scale of 1 to 10, how high a priority is this subject on the prospect's to-do list? If it's not a 9 or 10, focus on higher-urgency issues. Find a way to shift the content's focus to more closely align with the prospect's highest priorities.

*(Continued)*

4. Is the content written from your prospect's perspective—or your company's?
5. Is the content product focused on or discussing issues important to your prospect?
6. Identify your hooks. Is your primary hook within the first two sentences? If not, it should be. Do you have secondary hooks to keep your prospects reading farther (e.g., subheads, bulleted lists, and questions they want answers to)?
7. Identify your call to action. This may be a hyperlink to another content resource, an invitation to sign up for a specific content series that allows you to ask two or three questions to build out your prospect's profile, or simply a "Contact Us" link. Make sure that when the prospect responds, the information he receives expands on the initial story you've shared.
8. Is there a story? Can the audience see themselves and their situations through your content? Or are you presenting facts and statistics as stand-alone statements that may not seem relevant?
9. How many jargon words did you use? Can you replace any of them?
10. What's the conversational component? Have you made it easy for your prospects to pass along your content to a stakeholder or influencer? Is discussion of the issue made easier by the style of your content?

Assess the potential of your content to compel the selected persona and segment to engage with your company by reviewing these tips. Your relevance and results will improve if you focus on these areas as an evaluation guide for all your content-development projects.

## Chapter 10

# Content Structure for Competitive Differentiation

Marketers are responsible for differentiating their companies from the alternatives. Differentiation must take place during every stage of the buying journey. Taking a stance to directly attack your competitors is a reactionary defensive move that usually backfires. Buyers simply don't like or trust companies that put down the competition. Focus on developing highly relevant and contagious content instead, and you won't even have to mention the competition—this is the way it should be.

The experience and partnership your company extends to your customers should be reflected in your eMarketing strategies. This is the real story you want to share. Focus on the many ways your company provides business value that your prospective customers can't get anywhere else. This is true competitive differentiation. Show your prospects the advantages they'll gain by working with your company. You may be selling a similar product as your competitors, but the way your company helps your customers to get the outcomes they want is the key to why you retain them over the long term.

Three types of contagious content are fundamental for establishing competitive differentiation—educational-, expertise-, and evidence-focused content. Each of these content types works to differentiate you from your competitors, and when combined, they reveal the overarching story of the business value your company provides. Contagious content carries your company's signature style, recognizable to your prospects and customers even without mentioning the name of your company or product offerings. Most important, contagious content makes a lasting impression. Being remembered and referred to as a valuable, trusted advisor gives you more credibility. When the time comes for prospects to buy, you'll be top-of-mind.

- *Educational content* focuses on what buyers need to know to be able to think strategically about how to solve problems or take advantage of new opportunities to move their companies ahead.
- *Expertise content* showcases the business value your company brings that your customers can't get anywhere else—even if a similar product is available down the street.

- *Evidence content* proves that your company walks your talk. It's focused on the results your customers have achieved in partnership with you. Not feeds and speeds—business results.

Notice that none of these three types of content is focused on your product or service offerings. The differentiation is in the expertise and knowledge you have and how you apply them to transform your customers' unique situations and improve their success. This does not mean that your products and services can't ever be mentioned, but it does mean that they're not the focus of contagious-content resources.


## EDUCATION—WHAT BUYERS NEED TO KNOW

Educational content sets the selling stage by delivering information that buyers need to know. Eighty-five percent of buyers highly value content that includes the latest in educational insights to help them make better decisions.[1] Frequently, the problem a prospect is tasked with solving is outside that person's core-competency area. Companies are shifting to do more with less. Their hierarchies are flattening, blurring roles in new ways. It's entirely possible that the best solution to a problem also includes innovations unfamiliar to the prospect. The common denominator is that buyers need to learn enough about available options, related advantages, and mitigating risk to feel confident in recommending a course of action to their peers, staff, colleagues, and ultimately, their boss. They need encouragement that their success is attainable by choosing to work with your company.

Thought leadership and the provision of knowledge that shapes the successful outcomes of your customers' projects deliver value. Offer knowledge your prospects don't have in-house. People are so busy keeping up with the speed of business today that they simply don't have time to think strategically. And even if they make the time, they often are seeking expert direction and insights to guide problem-specific thinking. You can be that expert.

You have the opportunity to educate your prospects and proactively help them to grapple with their make-or-break priorities. With automation technology and contagious content, you can be the expert and long-term partner your prospects are seeking. Ultimately, this is what engagement is all about.

Educational content is exploratory. It often takes the best analyst insight and research, blends them with your company's unique approach and knowledge, and laces them all together with examples of how you've helped power success. This is the kind of content that gives your prospects ammunition to influence others—talking points for meetings, peer conversations, and presentations to their bosses.

Educational content helps to make your prospects smarter. It's not thinly veiled information focused on getting the sale but truly helpful information they can trust to be credible. As your prospects become smarter, they gain confidence. And if you're the first to influence their thinking, your company becomes the anchor. You become the trusted advisor your competitors have to work to unseat. This is why nurturing longer-term leads is so important. When nurturing is executed with educational content, you're positioning your company for the ultimate buying decision. Prospects learn, and you build trust. It's a win for both of you.

The most common type of educational content for B2B complex sales is white papers. However, great traction is being made during nurturing by leveraging topical article series and e-books, as well as by varying the delivery format to include written, audio, and visual options. People's attention spans are shorter, they multitask more often than not, and they learn differently. It's wise to keep these realities in mind because they can have a high degree of influence over the ways people respond to your educational content.

Pass-along value is also critical. With consensus groups for B2B complex sales ranging from 6 to –21 people,[2] it's necessary to educate a variety of stakeholders—all with different priorities for the project. For example, the finance executive will want to know total cost of ownership, whereas the line-of-business manager is more concerned with bottom-line revenues and profitability. By addressing the informational needs of all the buyer personas within the buying group, you'll accelerate your sales cycles as you facilitate consensus.

## EXPERTISE—WHY YOUR COMPANY IS THE HIGH-VALUE CHOICE

People turn to experts when they are faced with complex problems. They turn to trusted sources that provide strategic value. To become that source, you have to know the business value your company delivers, as perceived by your customers. This means what your company does, why, and the way it does so.

Generate stories that individually and combined express your experience and knowledge by using your unique expertise as the foundation of your eMarketing content plan. Each content resource will offer highly relevant insights which resonate with your prospects —one feeding into the next to extend your company's storyline.

Educational content is focused on showing your prospects why change is necessary for success. Expertise content demonstrates how your company's unique approach enables customers to make that change successfully to improve business results. Progress your prospects farther along in their buying process by using both content types hand in glove. A consistent focus on your business value keeps your content on track

### *Define the Business Value Your Expertise Produces*

To ensure consistency in your expertise content development, the business value you deliver must be applied to the perspective of each persona you address. Their viewpoints will vary, so make sure you step into the shoes of one persona at a time when you answer the following questions:

- What do you sell? (Not your product.)
- What problem does it solve for your customers?
- What does it ultimately help your customers achieve?
- What's the unique intellectual capital behind your company's approach?

Take a look at how what your company does helps your customers achieve strategic outcomes differently from other providers of similar products. Apply those principles to your contagious content development, and you'll find higher engagement because you've focused on the "What's in it for me?" your prospects want.

## EVIDENCE—LET YOUR CUSTOMERS DO THE TALKING

Evidence content uses third-party sources to validate that your company can indeed do what you say it can. Evidence content solidifies the credibility you've started to gain. This type of content includes customer success stories and testimonials, analyst reports that feature your company as a leader, endorsements by recognized industry luminaries, and in-depth research reports that back up your assertions. It also includes online commentary expressed by others about your company. Notice that much of this content is not within your control. But you do have the ability to make it available and easily found.

Customers are the best salespeople you have. People want to know that you've accomplished what you've promised for companies like theirs. Whether by size, industry, or problem, your prospects will move faster when there's evidence that what you say is credible. Prospective buyers are really looking for evidence provided by independent sources, not your own claims. Think about it this way: When you go to buy a car, do you rely on what the dealer says, or do you read the experts' opinions in *Consumer Reports* or consult online reviews by people who have purchased that vehicle?

Customer success stories are the best evidence you can present. Used correctly and pervasively, such success stories form the foundation that triggers your prospects' motivation for purchase. The key is to make your customer success stories about the success, not about company messaging.

A company-focused case study may be a validation point to push an end-stage purchase decision, but it's not compelling enough to drive early momentum and generate extended interest. Great testimonials are expected; therefore, their impact is somewhat diluted. After all, if they were bad, would you publish them?

A customer success story, on the other hand, is all about your customer. And if you want to get as much traction as possible, consider writing multiple stories from different angles and personalizing the stories to match the needs of specific prospect segments, problem-to-solution scenarios, and stakeholders.

### Tips for Customer Success Story Creation

Here are some tips to transform customer projects from case studies into success stories. Don't forget along the way—it's all about your customers.

**Setup: Can Your Prospects See Themselves in the Customer's Shoes?** A good success story sets up the description of who the customer is in a way that prospects can relate to easily and quickly. Done well, customer success stories empower your readers to visualize themselves in the situation as if it were their own.

**Action: How Did the Customer Solve the Problem, and How Did You Contribute?** Yes, the success story should include an exposure of the expertise your company applied to the customer's problem. (Notice I didn't say *product*.) Talk about how you worked with the customer to help them choose, accept, and facilitate the change. You also can include other avenues considered and show why they weren't chosen. This is a soft way to close the door on competitors without ever mentioning them or taking a negative stance. Position this part of the story as helping your prospects evaluate pros and cons. Remember to keep the focus squarely on the customer and their benefits, even though you're showcasing your company's expertise.

**Outcome: What Impact Did the Change Have on Your Customer's Business?** This section focuses on success. How did your customer's business outcomes change for the better? What other side benefits did your customer get? What new opportunities were available for growth that didn't exist before the solution was implemented? Were there any impacts beyond the expected that added to the residual value? If you use statistics as percentage improvements, make sure that they're easily understandable and related to the story. And make sure they matter to the audience.

**Sidebar: Display Product Components**   If you have to mention products within the story, do so sparingly. If the story is relevant to your readers, they'll want to know what was included in the solution to generate those results—so tell them. But don't distract them from the story by putting product names with trademark symbols and services marks throughout your text. Make sure the product sidebars are focused on value and benefits to them, not on feeds and speeds.

**Who: Use Different Perspectives to Add Traction**   If possible, speak with several different stakeholders who had vested interests in the project. Write success stories from each perspective to match your own prospects with diverse personas. People want to read about people like them who have the same concerns they do about problem and solution impacts. Success stories, just like content, are not at their most effective when written as one-size-fits-all resources. By creating customer success stories from the perspective of each contingent involved in the purchase decision, prospects will be able to see themselves being successful by following that same path. It's also worth noting that when you create content in this way, you're providing talking points that help all the people involved in the purchase decision discuss your company's solution as a viable choice.

## SALES CONVERSATIONAL BRIEFS

It's important to note that success stories also can be recreated as conversational briefs for use by your salespeople. You know the issues that are top-of-mind with your prospects. Your salespeople can supply you with the questions that prospects ask them during meetings. Break apart your customer success stories to extract answers with impact your salespeople can be prepared to use to forward prospect conversations.

---

**FIVE TIPS FOR CONVERSATIONAL BRIEFS**

1. Convert the sentencing used in textual success stories into conversational snips salespeople can easily weave into the discussion.
2. Include context that enables salespeople to discuss the statistical outcomes in ways that address specific segment interests.
3. Provide recommendations for related content salespeople can offer that extends the value of the conversation.
4. Add insights not included in the public version of the customer success story to enable salespeople to provide the "inside story."
5. Organize the conversational snips by setup, action, and outcome to make them easy for salespeople to refer to quickly.

---

## DealerOn—Contagious Content in Execution: A Case Study

In mid-2007, Navid Azadi, CEO of DealerOn, Inc., knew that he needed to increase the reputation and credibility of his company to create a higher level of sustainable growth. His vice president of marketing, Amir Rezvani, was certain that the way to achieve this outcome was through online marketing. Since DealerOn provides marketing Web solutions and tools to automotive dealerships, leveraging online components to connect with prospects made sense. The problem was that automotive dealerships, in general, were still focused on the traditional ways of selling. Many dealership executives hadn't yet come to understand the value for both their dealerships and their customers that an integrated Web solution could generate.

DealerOn chose to focus its online marketing with the goal of sharing expertise to elevate the company from a respected vendor to a thought leader within the industry. The company understood the value of spreading ideas across the Internet to connect with its prospects and enhance the relationships it enjoyed with its customers. With this goal in mind, the company rewrote its entire corporate Web site to focus on educational and expertise content that spoke to its customers' needs, not just about the company. The company selected a number of customers and interviewed them to develop customer success stories to show prospects the strategic benefits of online demand generation. The company also created a content-development plan to continuously publish fresh content to its Web properties.

But the company knew that its corporate Web site wasn't enough. To extend its reach, DealerOn implemented a blog with a twice-a-week publishing schedule. Blog posts were designed to share valuable insights, links to other relevant expertise, and generally educate prospect and customer audiences about timely issues. DealerOn also engaged with the few (at that time) noted automotive marketing bloggers, commenting on their blogs and encouraging interactive dialogue by writing posts that extended the thoughts and ideas of those bloggers.

DealerOn saw the traffic on its DealerRevenue.com blog double in less than a month as a result of the shift in the style of its content and adhering to a disciplined publishing routine. The company continued to grow and develop the blog and prove its value as a growing source of traffic for its corporate Web site and demand generation. Over 9,000 people viewed in excess of 15,000 posts on the blog over the last year.

DealerOn also had a large database of dormant prospects collected over time. Part of the company's eMarketing strategy was to clean the list and reengage those still interested. The company managed to reignite the interest of 30 percent of its dormant leads, tracking their activity and moving them forward in the purchase process. At the same time, the company wanted to evolve its existing customer relationships and launched a complementary e-newsletter to share thought leadership articles, cross-sell offers, and the personal touch of a column written by the CEO. The newsletter also served to introduce key staff members to the customers they interfaced with regularly but hadn't met personally. In addition, the newsletter shared instructive success stories to help customers get the best results possible from using DealerOn's solutions. These efforts have reduced the customer attrition rate to consistently below 5 percent, a highly beneficial outcome during economic uncertainty in the automotive industry.

When reflecting on the outcomes of DealerOn's first eMarketing strategy, Navid Azadi says: "Over time, our consistent delivery of customer-focused content has solidified our brand and reputation within the industry. Our eMarketing strategy has helped us evolve and formalize our brand's promise and value proposition, as well as segment our target markets and help us better visualize our ideal customers. We're moving steadily forward to evolve our eMarketing strategy as the catalyst for the growth of our company."

DealerOn has grown staff by 32 percent to meet increased demand and to better serve its customers. The company continues to work tirelessly to share new strategic ideas with its prospects to help them discover the need for its services before they even know what DealerOn really does. The feedback and learning the company received from its efforts has enabled it to create a comprehensive new tool to help its prospects and customers diagnose their needs across their entire online sales process. And finally, dealerships are increasingly getting on board with the value of Internet sales and marketing practices, which is good news for DealerOn.

## Chapter 11

# Create Content to Increase Attraction Value

When you motivate prospects based on an understanding of their catch factors—even amid an informational blizzard—your content will get their attention. This same principle applies to every communication between you and your prospects, whether through e-mail, Web search returns, blog posts, or your Web site. Initial impressions are the gateway between you and your prospects—and catch factors will get you through.

*Catch factors* are the preferences and aversions that form a lead's "gut reaction" to your communication. They help to determine whether you attract your audience's attention—or not. These factors include split-second assessments about their urgency for your information (e.g., does it apply to a real problem they have right now), whether or not you can impact their professional success, the effort required to access and process the information, and finally, their perception of your company's reputation and intent. The importance a recipient places on each of these five catch factors affects the attention you get—and the downstream revenue results.

According to Deidre Wilson and Dan Sperber's *Relevance Theory*, an individual draws a conclusion based on the first relevant meaning recognized and the one that requires the least effort.[1] This is where our millisecond attention spans come into play and why your marketing story needs to be relevant and compelling—at first glance. Leveraging the five catch factors helps you acquire attention and accelerate your prospects' related buying behavior.

Always remember that you're marketing to real people. Catch factors keep you from falling into the trap of evaluating your eMarketing content based only on surface demographics. To attract attention, remember that the director of information technology, the vice president of sales, and the line-of-business manager are all human beings who respond based on individualized perceptions and needs. Each of your potential buyers applies and assigns catch factors within seconds of viewing your content or communication.

## URGENCY—WHY YOUR MESSAGE IS IMPORTANT—NOW!

Urgency is all about your prospects—how important your information is to them, whether it solves a problem they have or is simply "noise." Don't confuse this factor with *your* urgency or a special time-sensitive call to action in your communication. The key to urgency is the degree of passion your prospects currently have about the topic of your messaging. This is usually associated with a problem they have to solve or a decision they have to make.

---

### DETERMINE THE SOURCE OF URGENCY

- Has a trigger event created a need for specialized expertise to quickly answer a priority shuffle?
- Are competitive advances threatening customer acquisition and loyalty?
- Have recent purchases been made because customers discovered their current system or process cannot deliver a critical business objective?
- Are deadlines forcing your potential buyers to seek alternative solutions?

These are all examples that affect urgency. Addressing them can increase "earned" attention.

---

Buyers are people who are change agents in their companies. They do their homework because they want to succeed. To build a business case that gains enough agreement to change the status quo, they first need evidence to prove their idea is the best choice. They're leaders passionate about generating particular business outcomes to help their companies succeed and grow faster than the competition.

Urgency is a primary driver in catching their attention. Collaborate with your salespeople to gather street-level insights that validate your prospects' need for what's offered in your communications and content right now, as well as in a few days or a week. If you discover their need is longer term, it's probably not worth it to prospects to pay attention at this moment. There are other, more urgent priorities in their lives making your information less valuable. Even if they determine the information might be useful at some future point, that communication still won't get more than their momentary attention. And when they're ready, they know new information will be available online.

One note of caution: Do not mistake a true case of urgency for frenzied activity. People are moving fast. Sometimes fast is just for the sake of fast. Make sure the issues you diagnose as urgent are actually about achieving business value. Otherwise, your messaging will miss.

The urgency catch factor is closely tied to your prospects' assessment of impact. Their need may have priority focus, but without an indication of impact, your communication won't be assessed as valuable enough to catch more than their momentary attention.

## IMPACT—WHAT'S IN IT FOR THEM?

Prospects have an ever-lengthening list of goals and initiatives they must manage successfully to deliver on business objectives and take advantage of market opportunities. This catch factor reflects your prospects' evaluation of the impact of your content in relation to their problem. Beyond the impact to their companies, prospects are concerned about the influence the outcome of their decisions will have on their professional standing within their company and with their peers and colleagues.

Your prospects are challenged every day to fix what's not working to move their companies, and themselves, ahead. Vague notions about nice to have but not critical benefits won't gain their attention. By demonstrating your company's expertise and ability to help them achieve successful outcomes, you increase their attention by addressing the potential impact to their initiatives and their careers.

---

### ADDRESS IMPACT WITH BUSINESS VALUE

- Illuminate contributions to increased revenues or decreasing costs.
- Expose future benefits.
- Highlight improvements to strength against competitors.
- Speak to the effect the outcome will have on your prospects' professional role.

For example, content about how automating processes can double their revenues has more impact for your prospects than an article about increasing efficiency.

---

Focus your content on communicating about topics prospects see as critical to success—and they listen. When the communication is all about them, their problem, and innovative approaches to solving it, including examples of others who have done so successfully—with your help, of course—you raise your company's value perception.

It's no longer enough just to have the product or solution that theoretically solves your prospects' problems. It's up to you to prove you can, why they should, and what they'll get. The more closely you tie evidence of related successful outcomes to your expertise, the more value you will be seen as providing. This also means your targeted customers will reap the residual benefits of wise engagement—both for their companies and for themselves.

## EFFORT—THE PERCEIVED ENERGY REQUIRED TO PAY ATTENTION

Effort manifests in your targeted buyers' evaluation of accessibility, time, and willingness to expend energy balanced against the perceived benefit of doing so. Is the information simple and easily absorbable? Is it straightforward or filled with terms, gobbledygook, and jargon that your prospects will have to work hard to understand?

People take the path of least resistance. Once they reach a conclusion, your opportunity to connect with them has been determined. If they perceive that paying attention to your communication is too costly in terms of effort, they will delete it, bury it under the paperwork on their desk, or otherwise ignore it. This is why setting expectations in your call to action is so important. Make sure that what they need to do to access and use your information is obvious. Eliminate barriers and hurdles that add to their effort. Make it easy for your prospects to take advantage of your expertise. Simplify their experience and the effort required to interact with your company.

---

### REMOVE EFFORT BARRIERS

- Develop content specifically for the audience.
- Simplify Web-page layout for instant relevancy.
- Apply context to statistics and comparisons.
- Make sure content has *scan* as well as *read* value.

---

Prospects expend effort toward your company incrementally. Whether they continue to pay the same or more attention is related to the experience they have with your information. If your targeted buyers decide to ante up their effort on your communication because you met their need for urgency and impact, make sure that it's easy to get value when they click.

Relationships are earned incrementally, so make sure the payoff for the effort your prospects expend goes beyond the expectations you set in your call to action. Consistency in providing information that delivers valuable and usable insights compels people to continue the dialogue. The right content sets your company up for prolonged and consistent attention from potential customers.

Given the daily deluge of information everyone endures, expect the effort catch factor to carry a lot of weight. Unless your company rates highly with the other catch factors, asking a lead to expend a lot of effort is an attention killer. A key component for enticing prospects to expend effort is your company's reputation.

## REPUTATION—WHAT'S KNOWN ABOUT YOUR COMPANY

Reputation is what your audience knows or thinks about your company. This catch factor is the first thing that comes to mind when prospects see your company name, logo, or product. How they perceive your company's "fit" in relation to their own needs is critical. The better a prospect's gut response to your brand, coupled with the perceived fit between your company and his, the higher the odds of catching his attention. Brand awareness drives the reputation catch factor, but it goes beyond simply knowing your company's name.

---

### ELEMENTS THAT CONTRIBUTE TO REPUTATION

- Customer success stories—especially for similar problem resolution
- Word of mouth by customers and peers—online or offline
- Search results—company, products, and keywords
- Media and analyst coverage
- Previous interactive dialogues held with your company

---

Reputation is earned or lost based on cumulative impressions. Consistency in the quality of your content eliminates conflicts and doubts that otherwise could cost you attention. Customer success stories and word of mouth increase your credibility with prospects.

Perhaps your prospect read an article you wrote that was posted on an industry Web site that she trusts. Or maybe your PR has been picked up in industry journals or on news Web sites they frequent. Your prospect could've just spoken with one of your customers at a networking event or conference. Reputation is earned incrementally in degrees of trust and credibility. The more competence and expertise ascribed to your company, the better your reputation.

Social media and user-generated content have enabled people to talk about their vendors with wide audiences. Marketers need to adopt tools that increase visibility into what's being said about their companies in the online places prospects frequent. Consider all the different ways your potential customers may have been exposed to your company, brand, products, and expertise. This can be different depending on which industry they're in, how you came to communicate with them, or how they came to know about you in the first place. Once you know what's being said—your company's real reputation—you can create content that evolves and expands the way prospects see your company.

Your messaging always should reflect the reputation you want to have in the minds of prospects when they hear from you—that of a vendor who is a knowledgeable expert in their field and a trustworthy partner. This is what gives your communications pull. Customer success stories have strong influence—people listen to other people's recommendations. The more evidence you provide where your prospects' peers are singing your praises—the stronger your brand reputation becomes within even a single marketing communication or content resource.

## INTENT—WHAT YOUR AUDIENCE THINKS YOU WANT

Intent depends on your prospects' perceptions of what they think you want from them. If they perceive you're focused on providing insights they find valuable, they'll be more compelled to pay attention. This includes the provision of new industry information, case studies show-ing how you've helped similar companies overcome similar problems, and even new research in an area of interest.

Conversely, if your message is a blatant or thinly veiled sales attempt, you risk alienating prospects with your obvious self-interest. Make sure your communication declares your intentions so that your prospects can quickly and clearly evaluate why you've contacted them. According to Stephen M. R. Covey in *The Speed of Trust*, "... we judge ourselves by our intentions and others by their behavior."[2] A straight-forward intent goes a long way in beginning a trusted relationship with your potential and current customers.

---

### YOUR COMMUNICATIONS PASS INTENTION SCRUTINY
### IF THEY ARE PERCEIVED TO

- Educate.
- Clarify issues.
- Offer information with little obvious gain to your company.
- Not request anything from your prospects beyond their attention.

---

When you share expertise with no obvious self-motivation, prospects see you as a vendor whose intent is to help them solve their problems and be more successful. Your prospects come to see you differently from all the others competing for their attention via self-interested pleas.

You also must be clear about your follow-on intentions. Inten-tion often depends on your prospects' evaluation of your company's authenticity and transparency. Make sure you give prospects what you've promised, with an emphasis on helping them learn or under-stand something they need to know. When your intentions are honest and supportive, you'll gain traction quickly.

Taken together, reputation and intent drive your prospects' reac-tions to your company. Their perception heavily influences your ability to catch and retain their attention. In combination with the other catch factors, the positive impact of intent motivates prospects to initiate dialogues with you about how you can help them.

## EXAMPLES OF HOW CATCH FACTORS CAN INFLUENCE BEHAVIOR

Catch factors can work together to influence your target market's interpretation and resulting behavior. Below are a few examples of activities that your prospects likely engage in today:

### *Example 1*

A prospect receives and immediately reads an e-newsletter from a vendor she considers an expert in resolving the types of problems she's facing.

**Reputation + Intent**   This vendor has earned attention through both reputation and intent. The information the vendor provides has a high value quotient that results in a worthwhile expenditure of effort for the prospect. The prospect has learned from past experience that the intent of the vendor is to be helpful, not trying to pitch a sale.

### *Example 2*

A prospect subscribes to a vendor's blog because one of the articles the company submitted to an industry portal gave them some useful insights. The prospect followed the link back to the vendor's blog and discovered a new and valued resource.

**Impact + Reputation**   The article on the industry Web site elevated the prospect's perception of the vendor's reputation. The results from using some of the tips presented in the article provided noticeable impact. The prospect visited the vendor's blog and saw useful information that validated his assumption that he had discovered a relevant informational resource. The opportunity to increase attention now lies with your blog's content.

### Example 3

A prospect uses a search engine to look for industry-specific information about a problem she is trying to solve. A link to your company's related Web page is in the first five search results. The description appears to relate directly to an explanation she thinks will be helpful. She clicks through.

**Urgency + Effort**   Being found in the first five search results reduces effort. Because your description is written to speak to the prospect's needs, she recognizes that you're addressing an urgent issue.

Once on your Web site, the prospect likes what she reads, but because she hasn't heard of your company before, she tries to satisfy other catch factors. In addition to the compelling content article, the Web page displays a related analyst report that lists your company as an expert in addressing the issue. You've now established a toehold on reputation. If a related customer success story is referenced on that Web page, you'll also have addressed the impact and intent catch factors.

As you audit your content with catch factors in mind, consider that they also can be embedded into your content and messaging design. You'll find that the nature of creating content focused on prospect needs helps you begin to address catch factors intuitively and helps to create higher relevance for your prospects.

## AN EXAMPLE OF CATCH FACTORS IN e-MAIL MESSAGES

Let's take a look at an e-mail example that doesn't use catch factors to engage the reader:

Hello Tom—
I've been trying to contact you regarding your interest in the business implications of social media, I have not heard back from you so I

assume you are quite busy, I understand how that is. So unless I hear from you, I will assume you have decided not to further investigate the possibility of implementing a social network community at your company.

This e-mail includes six uses of the pronoun *I*, showing that the focus is all about the sender. It's written in two long sentences. The message starts off by trying to make Tom feel bad because he's been unresponsive. It moves on to make assumptions about Tom and closes by cutting off the possibility of future dialogue.

Now let's look at an e-mail that uses catch factors to advantage:

Hello Tom—
Your new VP of Sales has some ambitious plans for increasing revenues this year. We've helped companies similar to yours improve customer acquisition by at least 9 percent with social media strategies.
I've got several ideas about how you can increase your close ratio.
May I have 15 minutes to discuss them with you?

This e-mail starts off by showing Tom that you've done your homework and learned about a priority he's dealing with. It uses four concise sentences and is direct and easy to understand. The e-mail addresses a triggering event and includes the five catch factors:

- *Triggering event:* Vice president of sales changed revenue forecast.
- *Urgency*—Has to be met this year, which gives it a likelihood of being top-of-mind priority.
- *Impact*—9 percent lift in deals—good for him, good for the company.
- *Effort*—Only asking for 15 minutes, and you've promised him ideas.
- *Reputation*—You've done your homework: similar customers and proof with the 9 percent.
- *Intention*—To share ideas, to help.

This message could be used as a voice mail, as well as an e-mail. It's conversational in style. It's focused on helping Tom become a star by empowering him to deliver impressive business results. And it promises that his 15 minutes won't be wasted because you've set his expectations for the dialogue.

## WHY CATCH FACTORS ARE IMPORTANT FOR TODAY'S MARKETERS

The long tail of Internet search is more powerful than ever. In Marketing Sherpa's survey of 478 B2B business product buyers, 80 percent stated that they found their vendor rather than the vendor finding them.[3] The quality and quantity of available Internet resources empowers buyers to find almost any information they need to make a decision. Today's buyers are quickly becoming very efficient researchers.

Your company's content must be available, as well as engaging. Your messaging must reach out and grab the reader's attention in a nanosecond. This is what catch factors do for you. Once you get the attention of your prospects, you have the opportunity to tell your story. You have the beginning of true engagement.

Figure 11.1 provides an example of questions your content should answer to get your prospects' attention. Figure 11.2 provides an example of how catch factors can be applied to developing content and communications. In relation to the priority on the top line—and the persona you're addressing—answer each catch factor question.

Put yourself in the shoes of your prospects, and think about how you want them to respond. Then use this figure as a guide for develop-

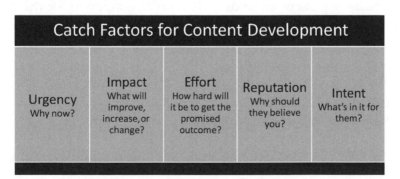

**Figure 11.1** Catch factors for content development.

| Your CIO Mandates Energy Reduction in Data Center by End of Qtr. | | | | |
|---|---|---|---|---|
| **Urgency** | **Impact** | **Effort** | **Reputation** | **Intent** |
| Optimizing your data center for energy use reduction can be accomplished in 6-8 weeks. | Upon completion you can expect up to 20% energy cost savings and no discernible change to user experience. | The energy savings package includes all labor for the installation and you won't have to explain or factor in any downtime for your end users. | We've implemented this energy savings package to 72 companies similar to yours successfully. | We provide 60 days of power use monitoring and interface with you to make sure your new system is optimized for best performance. |
| **Buyer Perspective:** The takeaway you want them to have. | | | | |
| I can solve this problem by my deadline. | I can make a noticeable impact with cost savings. | Implementation won't cause any interruption to the business. | These guys know how to make me look good. | They'll stick around to get the kinks worked out. |

**Figure 11.2**  Apply catch factors to content.

ing a content article to ensure relevance. It's possible to pull a number of topics from your worksheet for content development.

Topic examples could include

- The innovations that enable a low-risk solution to reducing energy costs
- The impact on the bottom line from optimizing energy savings
- The need to tune performance for increased savings after the implementation

Use the worksheet to keep prospects' concerns and takeaways top-of-mind while you develop your content. This method is extremely helpful for ensuring that your content is customer-focused, with relevance to your audience front and center.

When we consciously evaluate catch factors, it's easy to get the impression that your audience whips out a checklist, but this isn't true. These factors are applied subconsciously, efficiently creating an instant overall impression. Leveraging catch factors in the appropriate ways attracts the attention of your prospects, driving initial interactions that evolve into an interactive conversation—and ultimately, revenue combined with a long-term customer relationship.

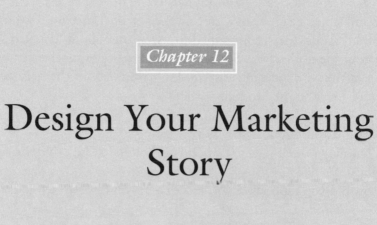

# Chapter 12

# Design Your Marketing Story

Marketing stories are the best way to attract today's informed buyers. Stories are best known as the novels we read, the fairy tales and fables we grew up with, and the personal anecdotes we share. In other words, they're ingrained in us. Stories about life events are what our memories save. Stories are what we tell ourselves to make sense of the world around us. We don't think about them as stories because we're so used to telling them.

- Why did you buy that snazzy new car?
- What did you tell yourself when you bought those pricey designer shoes?
- How did you rationalize those cool seats on the 50-yard line?

Everything people do is backed by a story they tell themselves to account for their actions. By harnessing the engaging nature of story format, your marketing programs will quickly lift your brand, company, and products to top-of-mind position. This means that your expertise has become the anchor against which your prospects will judge all other related input.

Stories are stealth marketing. When you enable people to step into your stories and envision their future with you—and their success—you develop credibility. Credibility leads to trust. Trust is the emotion on which complex business decisions are based. Trust is the prerequisite for progressive engagement.

Stories also help you to debug your message. Stories eliminate the effort it takes for your prospects to apply your information to their situations. The context of customer-focused stories invites dialogue because they're instantly relatable. In a recent blog post, Seth Godin wrote, "The challenge for marketers is to figure out how to change the story they are living so that their customers can change the story they tell themselves."[1]

Feeds and speeds about your products make it hard for prospects to tell themselves a story about how you can help solve their problems. By putting those facts into a relatable context (i.e., a story), you transform the reception and motivate your prospects to take follow-on interactions to find out more.

A story is like taking a break from the noise your prospects and customers encounter every day. Compelling marketing stories paint a picture of your prospect's world. Through words, you share their experiences, understand their challenges, and encourage their success. You provide a light at the end of the proverbial tunnel. Stories create a lasting visual impression in the minds of prospects. This is so because good stories are all about them.

## THE SIGNIFICANCE OF STORIES

A marketing story, by its very nature, is about someone like your prospect. This means that if you're communicating to a vice president, you write from his perspective—as a peer or colleague would talk with him.

Focus on segments, and tune your messaging to each persona. Buyers and influencers may be focused on solving the same problem, but their interests, perspectives, and even their vocabularies are different. The urgency they assign to various issues will be different, and their interpretation of benefits will be skewed based on the role they carry in the project.

A marketing story engages because it's situational and active. It's not just information about a product that talks about facts. A story shows buyers how to think about and consider an issue, the options for addressing it, and how they will get to a desirable outcome. Just as fictional stories are about a character seeking a goal, a marketing story is about your buyers solving a problem. If prospects see themselves in your story, they are more inclined to initiate a dialogue. You've shown them how to solve their problem. They "see" themselves as doing so successfully.

A story leverages both logic and emotion. Without emotion, the audience has no attachment. They can easily walk away. Once they're done with your factual message, it's likely they will forget it. Think back to college. I'm sure you remember studying facts in a textbook for an exam. How hard did you have to work for recall? Now think about that one professor you had whose lectures you could remember at exam time. It's likely the professor employed stories in how he taught. By applying context to factual information, your professor made it easier for you to learn and to keep that information top-of-mind.

People remember stories because they stir emotions. Stories have the ability to make us feel hopeful, to encourage us to try harder, and motivate us to succeed. When your stories engage emotions, people start spinning them to fit their own situations. Once a buyer inserts herself into a story, her brain spawns ideas of its own based on her unique circumstances. Your audience may well think they've arrived at the conclusion on their own, but they'll also relate that conclusion to you. This makes you the anchor on the subject and the first one they'll contact.

## STORIES INSTIGATE MOMENTUM

Stories, by their very nature, progress from beginning to middle to end. Your marketing story should unfold in the same way. It should compel prospects to continue with the story in step with their buying process. Figure 12.1 shows an overarching story parallel to the buying process.

The point is that stories move. Things are happening. The protagonist has a goal, overcomes conflict, and gets to the happily ever after. In business terms, the buyer has a problem to overcome to achieve a strategic objective. Not so different.

Stories link ideas. This is a key factor for your content strategy. As stories evolve, they build from one idea or premise to another. Stories

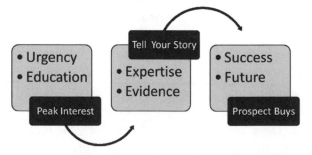

**Figure 12.1** Stories stimulate buying.

pull buyers forward in the buying process. For example, a story about technology innovation in a certain area builds from a vision to a reality when the follow-up story shows an early adopter's success using just that kind of technology. The first story planted the seed of desire, and the second story confirmed it as a possibility. Stories establish your company's credibility, showcase impact, and allow buyers to envision their own success through your eyes.

Your buyer synopsis is the foundation for developing relevant and engaging marketing stories. Break the problem-to-solution journey into pieces that can be used throughout the stages of the buying process. Make sure that there's a tie-in to the story that came before and a future story for continuity. This sets expectations and, when done well, builds anticipation. Roll out your story in a way that helps prospects build their knowledge, expand their horizons, and turn potential into reality.

### The Power of a Story in Action

An IT systems manager for a major medical facility needs to roll out network patches faster than he can today. For him, it is critical to protect computing devices from vulnerabilities that could expose patient information. Manually building patches from the software provider and deploying them to over 3,000 computers currently takes seven days and several IT engineers.

The manager turns to the Internet and commences research to find out how to improve his situation. He learns that a number of software tools are available to automate his patching processes. After reading an article he found from your company that discusses the benefits of automating the management of endpoints, he visits your company's Web site. Given the expertise and customer success stories he's found from your company, he believes that he can save well over 200 personnel-hours for a patch deployment. He also learns that your system can tell him which machines still might be at risk after the patch is deployed. Suddenly, he's hopeful about the opportunity to achieve a successful business outcome. Armed with your stories, he convinces the other stakeholders in the project to put your company on their short list.

Then the step-back happens. Your buyer slams the brakes on as he starts to question how easy this change is really going to be. How does he know that his expectations will be met?

This concern doesn't halt momentum because you've prepared for this possibility and are ready with a white paper that discusses the innovative technology that enables the solution to the prospect's problem and the ability of your software to play nice on any platform. You've also got another customer success story that emphasizes the ease of implementing the system. You've now shown the buyer testimonial proof that the solution can be implemented in less than six weeks. The buyer sees that he can well manage his side of the requirements. All the *i*'s are dotted and the *t*'s are crossed. He's back to visualizing happy days and how he'll shine professionally when the project comes off without a hitch.

Wait just a second. The CIO is concerned that the new system won't adapt to the corporate compliance policies and thinks that the total cost of ownership is too high. Not to worry, you assure your buyer and whisk him a customer success story that highlights the time savings achieved with your software and validates the customization capability that will enable the buyer's company to map to its compliance policies. Now that the step-backs have been answered and validation for his choice has been provided—specific to his CIO's concerns—the buyer commits to becoming a customer.

You may not be selling IT software, but it's likely that this ebb and flow—from positive to hesitant—exists for your prospects. You can eliminate hesitation by mapping your content to the buying process and developing stories to handle each step. Stories help you to elevate trust, with each relevant, timely communication moving your prospects smoothly forward in their decision to buy from your company.

## DESIGN CONTENT TO CREATE MINDSHARE

An old and true sales adage is to never talk about yourself in the first call. You'd just be giving prospects a way to say no. Instead, you ask about them; talk about their situations, showing you understand; and gather information so you can tune your communication for the next call.

The same is true for marketing. If I walked up to you, introduced myself, and proceeded to tell you all about me, would you be riveted to the conversation? Most likely you'd be looking over my shoulder to find the nearest escape. And this is exactly what prospects do when your communications and stories are all about you. They look over your shoulder for a more interesting story.

Creating mindshare is directly proportionate to your ability to stimulate curiosity and then deliver ideas that answer the curiosity with demonstrable results. The good part of the equation is that people are naturally curious. The difficult part for companies is that people are naturally curious about things that are interesting to them. Your company's products are an aside.

Stories that share valuable ideas are narrow and deep. Catch attention with one solid idea written to your prospect's perspective, and build on that idea by adding components that spin the idea outward from its core.

In Figure 12.2 you can see how your story begins with one focused idea. As you add layers, the idea expands along with your prospect's ability to grasp the impact and visualize how the idea or topic applies to his situation. The more you develop content that enables prospects to quickly and easily visualize the impact of your story and your idea, the faster you'll grab mindshare.

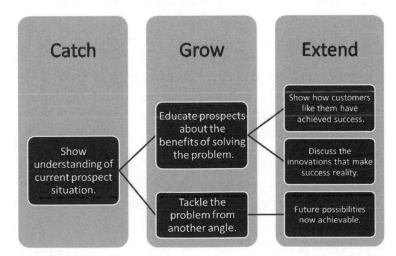

**Figure 12.2** Layer your story.

In fact, the more you invite your prospects to interact with you about their situations and your ideas, the more value your prospects will receive. As this interaction enables them to shape your ideas to address their specific situation, they will actively seek to learn more. Content that's built with layers makes it easier for prospects to align your story with their own.

When you build your story around a situation that reflects theirs, your prospects can easily step into it and participate. They can see themselves as the subject of your story and relate your customers' experiences to their own. Each story layer will make solving their problem easier. Stories simulate movement. Mapped to their buying process, your stories can pull buyers smoothly forward.

## AUTHORIAL STYLES—WHICH TO USE WHEN

The voice and tone of your content will create differing levels of engagement and response among your prospects. When you select an authorial style, it's important to consider what you want your prospects to think as they read.

Each type of content commands an authorial style. Whereas a white paper is indicative of expertise and is written with a professional tone, a blog post is written to be conversational in nature. An educational article falls somewhere in between. Your company's brand and culture also will determine, to a certain degree, the different styles of communication you embrace.

Your audience is the primary means for determining an authorial style. Engineers respond better to a more technical style. CFOs respond better to statistical proof points for costs and value. Your market segment also will dictate the use of jargon (sparingly), industry-specific acronyms, and technical terms. The better able you are to match your authorial style to your audience's perspective, the higher level of engagement you'll establish.

### *Examples of Authorial Styles*

Authorial styles match the types of content that motivate prospects to buy: education, expertise, and evidence.

**Mentor**    As a mentor, you're taking the educator approach. Your goal is to share the knowledge that teaches your prospects about the advantages of solving their problems in specific ways. Educating involves helping your prospects explore an unfamiliar course of action. You want them to know you have the answers to their questions. This style is friendly but firm, with a confidence of expression that encourages your prospects to learn more. The content focuses on their current problems and how to go about solving them with real-world examples.

The following excerpt from an educational article shows the mentor style. The article is about the ability of companies to find and use corporate knowledge assets to drive success. The company's product is never mentioned, only what it enables.

> The lack of information visibility on demand impacts the entire enterprise. Operational efficiency is important, but executing strategy in the best way possible is the elemental key to your company's success. And, with the improvements in enterprise search technology to enable intuitive information access across disparate repositories, there's no reason why your company shouldn't reap the rewards of better strategic decisions, made faster.

**Thought-Leadership Expert**    When showcasing your company's expertise, you are sharing information that drives the innovations that improve the value your products deliver to your customers. As an expert, you apply those innovations to address industry trends with a strategic focus. The material is higher level and helps your prospects envision what their futures can be like with your company helping them to achieve higher levels of success.

The following excerpt is from a thought-leadership article that shares expertise about application virtualization. This is a concept the company's prospects were beginning to embrace. The style is professional without being overly academic or trying to sell.

> Application virtualization affords IT the ability to truly isolate applications without impacting user productivity. When a user needs two versions of an application, most operating systems say no. But with

the capability to easily package up each version to run without impacting the operating system, users can run multiple versions side by side, easing their frustration and keeping them on task.

The beauty of sandbox isolation is that it can be done with zero-footprint install—meaning no need for drivers, back-end servers, or desktop agents. And, when you're not actually installing anything on the individual device, the chances for compatibility issues are eliminated.

**Peer**   When using evidence to validate that your company is effective at solving problems similar to those of your prospects, a peer authorial style carries weight. One of the best formats in which to consider using a peerlike authorial style is a customer success story. Customer success stories about companies similar to your target market developed with a peer authorial style are more compelling than if they were written with the company's voice. When you focus your customer success stories to read as a peer talking to a peer, the connection the story establishes with your audience increases because they feel a kinship with that customer's story. It's likely that they can relate to the situation, the challenges, and then visualize the successful outcome as their own.

The other great use for a peer authorial style is in a blog. People expect to glimpse the person or personality behind the writing. Blogs are conversational in style. The writing is more casual, even if the topics are serious. The best blogs also educate and throw in a bit of controversy to get people talking.

The following excerpt is from a blog post I wrote back in April 2007. It still pulls a high readership and is an example of a peer authorial style. It's casual, with a bit of humor, but focused on providing insights that readers value.

> For some reason, it seems there's a belief that people don't actually *read* online content. Well, thanks to research by the Poynter Institute's Eyetrack study, we now know that's untrue. Who knew?

Matching authorial styles to your audience, format, and media expectations bolsters the impact of your communications. As you shift your authorial style to accommodate the variety of needs within your audience, you may find it worthwhile to revise your existing content to reflect styles. This is especially true if your company's existing content is all written in a company voice and focused on the company and your products. Your current materials probably provide a great foundation for creating contagious content quickly to accelerate your move to compelling eMarketing.

## QUICK GUIDE TO WRITING A MARKETING STORY ARTICLE

Writing a marketing story article isn't rocket science. Choose a process that helps you to generate consistently valuable stories that produce a high degree of engagement. The steps below lay out a simple process for creating one type of marketing story.

### Step 1: Select a Problem and Topic for the Article to Address

The subject should match a top-of-mind priority. When considering options for your stories, think narrow and deep—not broad and shallow. You need to put meat on the bones of a marketing story.

### Step 2: Decide Who You're Writing To

Determination of the audience will set the type of writing, phrases, and terminology you'll use to connect and will guide you in addressing impact. Because you're now writing to someone specific, this also will help you to frame intent so that it's clear and acceptable to that person. Remember to keep the jargon to a minimum and choose words considered relevant and meaningful to your audience.

Depending on the number of people in the consensus group—usually at least seven—you may want to write several versions of the article, focusing each on meeting the needs from a different perspective.

### Step 3: Choose an Approach

Now that you know your topic and who you're audience is, choose an angle from which to address the subject matter you've selected in a way that plays well with your expertise. Once you have your approach, make sure the style you use and the way you write about the topic tie into your company's essence. Build your company's reputation and elevate your credibility with potential buyers by ensuring that your content ties in with your expertise.

### Step 4: Outline Related Reasons, Options, and Outcomes

In this step, you're going to address the impact for your audience. Establish a natural flow for your story by following the reasons, how they play into the options, and arriving at the outcomes. When you make the list below, keep in mind who you're writing to, the topic you've selected, and the angle of your approach.

### List

- Three reasons why eliminating this problem is important
- Three options for how to ideally solve the problem
- Three outcomes the prospect can expect to achieve when the problem is solved

You may be asking, "Why three?" Three is a concept people relate to almost subconsciously—morning, noon, and night; beginning, middle, and end; crawl, walk, and run. Because we're so used to it, we've come to expect concepts to be delivered in threes. If there are three parts to something, buy-in to the story feels natural because the order of things is honored and doesn't even need to be mentioned. Very rarely do people differentiate unless the structure of the piece is more or less than three (such as the previously mentioned "Five tips to...," "Top 10...," and "Seven habits of..." examples).

### Step 5: Write Your Story Article

In consideration of today's time limitations, plan for a completed article of 650 to 900 words. Choose your authorial style. Show respect for prospect attention and reduce the effort necessary to engage with your story by limiting the article to around five minutes of read time. More "carrot" than "stick" in phrasing can increase engagement.

# Expand Story Impact with Amplifiers

You've done the work to know your prospective buyers. You've got an eMarketing strategy in development and are mapping content into your plan. You're interviewing customers and writing stories that bring the value of your company and its solutions to life with compelling real-world scenarios. Now let's explore how you can expand your stories by increasing their impact on accelerating your prospects' progress.

Amplifiers help you structure your content to confirm, correct, or expand information and knowledge prospects need to actively engage with your company. By designing your content with attention to amplifiers, you'll naturally address concerns to keep your prospects moving forward.

## THE NATURE OF AMPLIFIERS

*Amplifiers* are guides that help you to tap into the natural ways prospects think by using emotional constructs. Since it takes multiple touch points to move a prospect forward in the buying process, amplifiers provide a number of ways to catch attention and keep prospects focused on your company's ideas and thought leadership.

These five amplifiers provide formats for creating content that answers emotion-based concerns to keep the buying process moving forward. This doesn't necessarily mean a purchase decision. Depending on the stage of the buying process, this decision could include a choice to engage with you to learn more, a download of a relevant white paper, or even a chance to blog about what they've learned.

---

### THE FIVE AMPLIFIERS

1. *Answer a question.* Address a question about a controversial subject.
2. *Relieve a doubt.* Alleviate concerns about the viability of success.
3. *Simplify complexity.* Use building blocks to tell your story across buying stages.
4. *Provide a path.* Map the process for your prospects.
5. *Mitigate a risk.* Make the choice to buy safe.

---

People want to know that their assumptions are correct. Until they are sure, they often choose to delay or make no decision at all. Amplifiers help you eliminate emotional constraints, both consciously and unconsciously, that slow the momentum of the buying process. By helping to release their emotional constraints, you gain the trust of your prospects, and this keeps them moving forward.

### *Answer a Question*

The secret is in addressing a question about a controversial subject that your prospect has top-of-mind. The more controversial the subject matter, the higher the degree of attention your communication is likely to get.

A controversial subject provides a prime opportunity for you to differentiate the way your prospect thinks about your company and the value you bring to her project. Just make sure that you can substantiate your claims.

So how do you know what's controversial? Talk to your existing customers. What's making them uncomfortable? What new questions do they have? What did they need to know as they decided to partner with you? Put yourself in their shoes, and consider both personal and professional implications.

Once you have your questions and stories, map them to the buying process—just as your prospect will experience them. Be sure to build out the story by placing it within a context that resonates with the prospect. Focus content on delivering the information the prospect needs to answer the question at hand. The series of questions you develop can become a topic list for a content series for each group of prospects. You also can cross-reference content for one profile in messaging to another to promote pass-along between influencers with different needs involved in the project.

Let's say that your prospects are asking themselves how they can build a business case for using a video game as an element of their training strategy. The question may be, "How can I be sure that video games actually help staff to retain the training to get up to speed faster than with traditional training methods?"

A message such as the following doesn't answer the prospect's most top-of-mind question—how to build a business case:

> Video games are truly transforming the business world. Games are being used to train, manage, and recruit new employees and are also being utilized for advertising and product placement purposes by advertisers seeking new mediums to reach out to their consumer audiences.

The following message is designed with a direct purpose in mind—to answer that top-of-mind question for the prospect.

> When training budgets are tightened, wouldn't it help if you can educate your staff about new products quickly, with better long-term retention? Our customers are using video games to accelerate that learning curve, getting their employees up to speed with an average reduction of 30 percent in time to proficiency.

The first message is a general message designed to cover all the bases about what video games can be used to accomplish. The second message is focused on answering a known question for a particular target segment. It's written more personally, is easier to engage with, and provides specifics that will motivate the prospect to want to learn more.

### Relieve a Doubt

When people begin to consider change, they often hesitate. Change brings uncertainty about potential options, professional ramifications, and whether the change will result in what they expect. Change also offers the opportunity for choice. And, as we all know, there's always more than one way to choose. So how do your prospects know that they're making the right choice?

Doubts come in many forms—from concerns about the viability of success to suspicions that the results competitors (or your company) claim to achieve can't be true. Misconceptions and misinformation can fuel doubts. Thanks to the Internet, there's a lot of misinformation available and myths being propagated. Proactively addressing the doubts your prospects encounter increases your credibility.

Define the potential concerns your prospects might have, and proactively answer them in your stories. Be subtle. Use examples that specifically show how other customers proactively alleviated that concern or were successful despite it. You also might assess how competitors play into the concern and apply your expertise in a different context.

Saving your prospects from future headaches by being the vendor who corrects a misunderstanding about a course of action further elevates your status during the buying process. Take a hard look at the misconceptions in the market caused by a lack of understanding by influencers or to just plain untruthful claims made by competitors. Don't be afraid to specifically address these misconceptions. Take a leadership stance, put the issue front and center on the table, and address it clearly and directly.

The beauty of this amplifier is that by proactively addressing potential doubts, you show that you understand the prospect's situation, escalate her confidence, and provide further evidence of your credibility. Doubts are natural. They're going to happen whenever change and choice are afoot. Relieving doubt strengthens the trust level between your prospects and your company. And that's just where you want to be when they're considering change.

Let's take a look at a company-focused example of a lead-in that doesn't catch attention:

> Our computing products provide significant benefits for preserving the environment by improving energy usage, eliminating harmful substances, and reducing material consumption.

Now let's look at a lead-in designed to focus on the prospect's concerns about dealing with a priority:

> You need to reduce network costs. Going "green" has appeal ... conceptually. But you can't afford to lose speed to save energy. We can prove going green won't cost you an ounce in productivity.

The first example is focused on the company's products and is too general to be immediately engaging. It could've been written for anyone. The message is great for the environment but says nothing about the issues that address the prospect directly.

The second message is an example of how you can target a message to a doubt you know your prospect may have. It begins with the payoff—reducing network costs. It then addresses a concern the prospect may have about diminished performance and offers proof that her concern can be alleviated.

### *Simplify Complexity*

Complexity in business is a given—and it's increasing. By mapping your content to the buying process, you have a strategy for breaking the story into building blocks that make it easier for prospects to assimilate change. With each story building on the preceding one, you empower your prospects to move forward by overlaying the solution onto their situation. You enable them to feel more control while they build the picture of an achievable outcome.

By breaking the complex down into simple, tangible steps or scenarios, you make your solution approachable. Simplifying puts your company into the position of a leader, an expert, and a trusted partner.

Instead of addressing how comprehensive your solutions are, highlight the individual values that are key considerations for your prospects in relation to the problem they're attempting to solve. Build your story as you show them how to weave those parts together to get the outcome they want. No one cares that your solution has gazillions of features unless each of them is relevant to the situation at hand.

By using a simple structure, you can create a series of communications that engages by increasing your prospect's comfort levels with each step. Simplicity is unique, highly desirable, and more easily embraced.

When applying the simplicity amplifier, take a look at what your messaging addresses. Anything that results in a list can be broken into separate messages that provide digestible building blocks for your prospects. Let's say that your messaging includes this sentence:

[Our company] is an all-inclusive, enterprise class community platform offering all levels of Web 2.0 technology from blogs, discussion forums and wikis, to social networking, to video and photo sharing, voting, rating, tagging, etc.

Often, marketing communications attempt to cover too much in one shot. This message lists 10 features of Web 2.0 technology included in the platform and follows that with *etc.*, which makes that list more daunting. The list is so extensive that it doesn't mean anything. Instead, consider creating a message that puts context around the outcome most desirable to your target segment—how easy it can be to establish an interactive online community:

Establishing and running a productive online community is delivering strategic business advantages to companies like yours. We'll help you make "build it and they will come" happen by combining the best interactive tools to encourage frequent member participation. It's easier than you may think.

In this example, we make the complex idea of establishing an online community sound simple and easy to do. We tackle the issue of participation—the most common failure point for online communities—and tell our prospects that they can derive outcomes advantageous to their business. And isn't that much more compelling than a list of features without context?

### *Provide a Path*

Simplicity upfront is what makes complexity easier to embrace, but so does showing your potential buyers how they'll get there. Map the process for them. By showing your prospects the logical steps it takes to get from beginning to end, you help them to envision themselves accomplishing the project successfully. You give them a concrete course of action that also helps to remove doubts.

This amplifier is used to great advantage toward the later stages of the buying process—after your prospects have bought into the idea of taking action. When buyers grasp the nuances involved in the process and see a well-defined course of action, everything becomes more simple and straightforward.

A how-to guide approach can help marketers address this amplifier. Consider all the steps of the project and prioritize them. By clarifying each step, you provide relevant insights that address high-value needs for prospects. You'll actively increase their confidence in themselves and in your company's solution. You'll also lower the perceived effort to implement your solution.

### Mitigate a Risk

Accompanying any big decision is the shadow of risk. None of us likes risk. In fact, it would be nice if it disappeared and made all our choices automatically the best ones. Since this is not likely to happen, helping your prospects mitigate risk makes you a preferable, trusted, and credible vendor—one not afraid of the tough stuff.

When confronted with risk, the three most natural responses are avoidance, transference, and reduction. Complex sales, by their very nature, come with risk. The key to this amplifier is to monitor your prospects for risk tolerance and to proactively step up to address the risk they've assigned the most concern. Show them how to avoid it or transfer it to you, or prove that you can reduce its potential impact.

Each stakeholder in the project will have different risk concerns. Each one should be addressed from the appropriate perspective. Your credibility goes up and resistance to choosing comes down once you've unified your prospects' confidence. I'd rather be in a boat with someone who can help me get to shore than with someone oblivious to a gash in the side of the hull. Wouldn't you?

When you're considering how to mitigate risk, don't forget about the prospect's professional risk. There's nothing like a healthy concern about taking actions that can jeopardize a career to dash your chances of getting a sale. Status quo is preferable to unmanageable risk. This needn't be an obstacle when you know that mitigating risk is as much a sales role as a marketing one. Customer success stories are a key to lowering risk perceptions because you're offering proof that the outcomes are viable and successful. Proactively addressing risk helps marketing to maintain momentum and build credibility throughout the buying process.

## FOCUS SQUARELY ON THE CUSTOMER

Many companies start out with all the best intentions in the world to be customer-focused. However, your company and your products are what you're immersed in every day and what you know best. It's intuitive for you to talk about them and how great they are. Amplifiers help you to focus your eMarketing content on the emotional constraints of your prospects and stop that slide back into company speak.

Get to know your customers—develop profiles, evolve them into personas, and then construct buyer synopses that you can use to actively get an inside view of your prospects' reality. Get a firm handle on industry trends, and look down the road. Understand your prospects' reality and proactively address it.

Proactively responding to unspoken concerns through the appropriate use of amplifiers will help your company to build engagement. Consistently using amplifiers in your content strategy execution will add momentum and anticipation to the dialogue between your prospects and you. With an eye to what's coming, eMarketing strategies can engage your prospects in addressing their current needs and realities while also showing them you've "got their backs."

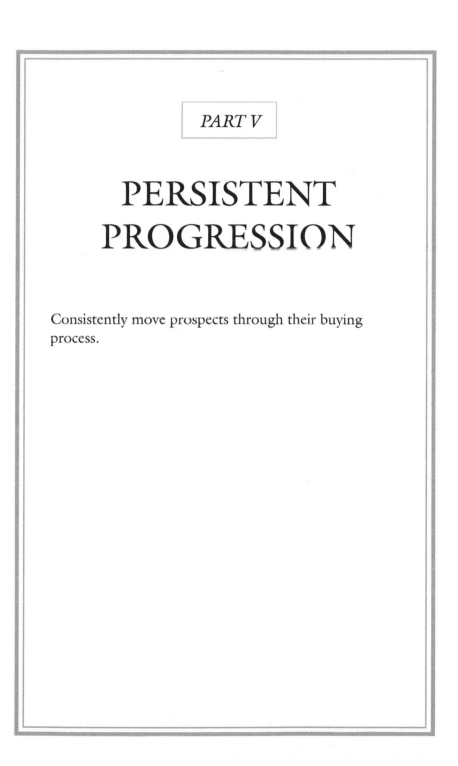

## PART V

# PERSISTENT PROGRESSION

Consistently move prospects through their buying process.

## Chapter 14

# How to Facilitate Prospect Progression

When asked, over half of B2B companies will tell you that they have a nurturing program in place. Half of them say that they have a lead management system in place. Yet 64 percent of executives say that they are dissatisfied with nurturing results.[1] It's clear that marketers still have more opportunity to increase their impact on downstream revenues. Developing an eMarketing strategy focused on progressively nurturing prospects to sales readiness is the answer.

With the right approach, you can consistently move prospects through their buying process until they are sales ready without expending precious sales time and energy. An eMarketing strategy that coordinates content and communications with technology will prove that generating sales-ready prospects is possible—as well as profitable.

Focus on producing consistent shifts throughout the buying process. Shifts are the incremental steps a prospect takes as he makes progress toward the decision to purchase. Match your content and communications to the evolving informational needs of your potential buyers and proactively orchestrate their progression.

The handoff of prospects to the sales force is a key transition and one that must be completed at the right time to optimize sales processes. Tossing raw leads "over the wall" has proven to be less than effective. What marketers need is a seamless process that tracks and promotes a prospect's progression through the buying process until he reaches a known readiness state—that he is informed enough to want to buy. This is when sales should get that prospect. Until then, nurturing is in charge.

## INTELLITACTICS INCREASES QUALIFIED DEMAND: A CASE STUDY

In 2007, Pam Casale, CMO of enterprise security solutions provider Intellitactics, was challenged to provide the company's sales force with fully qualified and well-informed sales opportunities—instead of raw leads. To accomplish this shift in responsibility, Director of Marketing Michaela Dempsey began exploring options for marketing automation to smooth the process. But the marketing team didn't just rely on itself. The marketing team involved the sales force in the design of their lead-qualification process. The company then chose to automate and monitor its marketing campaigns with the integration of its Salesforce.com CRM system with a Manticore Technology solution.

eMarketing processes and the underlying technology provide a great opportunity for marketing and sales alignment. When you're relying on virtual behavior to determine the level of prospect interest, you need to work with sales to jointly agree to the indicators of sales-ready interest. After analyzing all the steps in the company's planned campaigns and discussing quality factors with the sales force, the Intellitactics marketing team agreed that the prospects who asked to participate in a specific combination of activities were the most qualified for a sales handoff.

Once they knew the ideal profile, Pam and her team defined the process to identify those prospects as they became qualified. Because the company's technology platform supported configurable activity-based scoring, marketing had quantitative data to identify a true prospect. Defining a lead historically had been a point of contention between sales and marketing. Automated scoring of prospect behavior removed that point of contention.

Marketing used a combination of content types, including sponsored analyst and expert research reports, Webinars, and blog posts promoted via automated e-mail campaigns. To quantify results, the marketing team also was empowered to track sales generated from marketing campaigns all the way through customer acquisition. Intellitactics realized return on investment (ROI) on its Manticore Technology solution within two months of implementation, demonstrating how powerful technology can be. Intellitactics was able to attribute six deals to their new system during their first year of using an automated marketing process—not to mention the 171 percent increase in sales opportunities actually accepted by sales into the pipeline.

By taking a closer look at the achievements of the newly created alignment between marketing and sales, you'll see that technology is a great enabler for a solid eMarketing strategy. Intellitactics is a mid-size company whose competitors are big guns like EMC Worldwide and CA. Due to limitations on available resources, as well as budget restrictions, competing head to head with marketing campaigns wasn't an option. Because the company is smart about how it tracks and uses prospect intelligence, Intellitactics is able to continuously increase the quality of the connections it makes in its market space.

Pam also found that marketing-educated prospects yielded a 200 percent higher connect rate from telemarketing follow-up calls. Telemarketing calls were used primarily to add personal touches during nurturing. By asking the right questions during these calls, Pam's team gained insights that enabled them to both tune their scoring process and discover the optimal time for personalized outreach. For example, Intellitactics learned that it had been waiting too long to interface personally with buyers, giving the company's competitors a chance to captivate prospects' mindshare. By adjusting the scoring process, salespeople began connecting at the right time.

Intellitactics has shortened its sales cycle by 30 percent with the added efficiency of a coordinated marketing and sales effort in support of a solid eMarketing strategy. Integration of the Manticore Technology solution with the Salesforce.com CRM system made it possible for the sales team to achieve better visibility into its nurturing activities. This, in turn, enabled the sales force to step in and take over a prospect relationship that might be progressing faster than the scoring system indicates.

Intellitactics' use of focused nurturing content also enabled the marketing team to progress more than 100 inactive leads to sales-ready status within 75 days. The team is also qualifying an average of 60 percent of its prospects, an increase from the 30 percent standard that existed before deploying the new system.

CMO Pam Casale says that her biggest challenge is the demand for the constant creation of content. In her first iteration of automated marketing campaigns, Pam used expert resources for content. She intends to develop an internal strategy for content creation as marketing evolves its ability to connect with prospects. Internally produced expertise content will position Intellitactics as a thought leader for its existing and future customers.

Short of being able to immediately generate its own expert-level content, Intellitactics realized that consistency in quality content was key to its eMarketing strategy. One of the ways Pam's team accomplished consistent exposure was by incorporating the content on the company blog into eMail campaigns and sponsoring Webinars on related subjects.

Telemarketing follow-up calls at midcampaign increased the connection rate by 200 percent—proving that consistency pays off. Can you imagine this happening if the company's prospects hadn't been exposed repeatedly to quality information that helped to set expectations and build credibility for the company? Second, sales cycle length has declined by 30 percent in response to the alignment between sales and marketing. Because salespeople had high visibility into marketing activities and prospect responses, they were able to step into the relationship without friction.

### TELL ME MORE . . .

One way to increase the velocity of the buying process is to get prospects to ask you to tell them more. The "Tell me more" concept was first leveraged through the serialization of stories told in segments over time centuries ago. The idea was to hook listeners and then leave them with a cliffhanger they had to wait for. The penny papers carried the tradition forward into more modern times, and even the *New York Times* has serialized novels. The ability to publish content easily in digital formats has enabled people to begin experimenting with serialization again. Stephen King wrote his novel, *The Green Mile*, as a six-part serial.[2]

Nurturing programs that accomplish the "Tell me more" outcome generally employ the principles of serialization. A nurturing program for a complex sale includes multiple touches. If you've planned your eMarketing strategy to include problem-to-solution themes, then each one of them can be implemented as a serial campaign. Each touch can carry forward from the last one and end with a cliffhanger that builds anticipation for the next message.

A series approach to content can simplify the challenge of content development with limited resources. Review your content map for a particular problem-to-solution theme as applied to the buying process. If you break one story into segments, you've got serialized content. A 4,000-word story can be delivered as one e-book or as a six-part series in your nurturing program. An e-book is downloaded and taken away by your prospects—marking the end of your insight opportunity—although the use of embedded hyperlinks is changing this to a degree. A series, delivered as online content with activity tracked by your marketing automation system, can provide a wealth of insight and visibility into buying patterns.

Serial content brings a wide range of benefits, including

- Consistency of relevance in content
- Increased search optimization for keywords and phrases
- Pass-along value that expands your reach and depth
- Setting and delivering on expectations
- Thought leadership development and recognition
- Increased company credibility

By including forward and backward links to tie all the pieces together, you can gauge when interest intensifies by tracking how the content is accessed. Prospects won't always follow your story in a linear fashion. Noting the point at which the story catches hold and compels your prospects to download the other pieces can help you to determine buying stage as well as interest levels. Of course, prospects who read each part of the series show a steady level of progressive interest. Either way, you'll gain valuable intelligence that will help you to perfect your serial-content efforts over time. Publishing a series also can help your company be seen as a reliable resource for specific expertise.

Figure 14.1 shows a simple example of how a serialized problem-to-solution content campaign can build an ongoing story that keeps prospects wanting more.

Below is a foundation for how a problem-to-solution content series might play out. Notice the threads running through the steps and how the focus is kept on the scenario, not the product. Storyline content can be generated from the ideas captured for each step. The keys to the "Tell me more" principle are to ensure that your topics hit the mark, share compelling clues about what's coming next, and provide access to the story pieces that have come before.

**Problem**   Prospect manufacturing companies have teams located around the world who need to collaborate on product design and innovations, working on large data sets in real time. They need to

| | |
|---|---|
| **Problem** | • What the problem is and why solve it. |
| **Step A** | • How this problem impacts their business. |
| **Step B** | • Explain the rewards of solving the problem. |
| **Step C** | • Why solving it now gives them an advantage. |
| **Step D** | • Future industry trends that add risk to not solving. |
| **Step E** | • How customers like them have solved the problem. |
| **Step F** | • Simplify the complexity of solving the problem. |
| **Solution** | • How your expertise delivers business value. |

**Figure 14.1** Problem-to-solution content series.

get products to market faster and ensure they're applying the best minds in their companies to each situation. When teams can't see and manipulate the data in real time, design is delayed, lengthening time to revenue. Companies also must protect their design information and ensure they always have the latest design data securely behind corporate firewalls.

**Step A:** The problem impacts prospects' business by driving up costs and lengthening design time, giving their competitors a better shot at getting to market first. Coordinating schedules, spending precious time traveling, and the associated costs reduce the frequency in which teams can work together in the same location. Manufacturing companies need an infrastructure that allows teams in remote locations to work with data in real time so they can leverage the best what-if scenarios to design their products better and faster. When modifications happen independently, remote team members are left waiting to receive the latest design modifications to offer response and feedback. This necessitates additional iterations to reach the final design.

**Step B:** When their prospects can enable all team members to see each other and the modifications made to design data in real time, no matter where they are, they shave valuable time off the process. They also get the best ideas in the "room" because everyone on the team is working with the same data together.

**Step C:** The window for profitability from new-product innovations is narrowing. Competitive advances necessitate that companies get products to market faster as customers demand impressive innovations, not just version improvements. Design expertise culled globally enables companies to retain and leverage the best minds in the world, no matter where they live. Combining cultural insights improves innovation.

**Step D:** Companies that don't continue to improve the way they collaborate on product design will be left behind. Blurring global boundaries offer expansion markets to first-mover companies. Data sets are only getting larger as products become more complex. Technology that improves visual and interactive use of data is becoming more readily available.

**Step E:** Customer A's design team was able to see a design flaw through manipulating visual data in real-time collaboration with global team members. Because the issue was resolved prior to prototyping, the company saved hundreds of thousands of dollars, shaved months off its time to market, and maintained first-mover advantages that increased profits.

**Step F:** The solution is transparent to users. Every team member will use the laptop or desktop familiar to them. The data is made available as if it resides on each person's computer. Each team member can manipulate the data with everyone else seeing the changes in real time. Because they're all in the same "room," interacting with the data together, new ideas catalyze faster, and mistakes are minimized. The result is reduced time to product innovations without the need for intensive retraining or complex solution deployment.

**Solution**   Now's the time to showcase the proof that your company delivers on what you've promised. Subtle incorporation of the following points will help your prospects see that the assumptions they've made about your expertise are true.

- With over 800 years of combined industry expertise, our specialists have helped manufacturing companies improve the way they use data to design and bring products to market in myriad situations.
- We hold the patents on a number of critical elements in our solutions.
- Because we designed the innovations, we know how to apply them to a wide variety of situations to generate the results our customers need.

One way to present this story is to use another customer scenario to evidence these points to keep this content from becoming an obvious company factoid.

## THE GIFT OF GOING WIDE

The right eMarketing strategy helps you reach beyond the decision maker to influence the other stakeholders involved in or influencing the project. Whenever I ask clients to describe their prospects, they focus primarily on a single decision maker. Yet consensus groups for complex sales include a number of people, even though only one of them is the ultimate decision maker. If you're only marketing to one of the people involved in the decision, you're depending on the decision maker to influence the other members of the group on your behalf. That's leaving a lot to one person.

The goals for going wide are to become the go-to resource for information that helps prospects to solve their problems while facilitating the conversation between stakeholders, enabling them to convince each other that your company is the best choice. Persistent progression depends on marketing's ability to facilitate these conversations.

eMarketing expands your reach and range to communicate with virtually anyone, anywhere, on their own terms. By building personas and using appropriate authorial styles, you can reach all the participants in the decision, supporting them in their roles from advisor to decision maker.

When you create a content series for the ultimate decision maker, consider the variations you'll need to have an impact on the other stakeholders you need to engage. The beauty of building your eMarketing strategies from buyer synopses is that it gives you the versatility to address stakeholders without adding a ton of complexity to the process.

However, going wide also means you really need to manage the process efficiently. First, your chance of success increases if you involve sales in the discussions about stakeholders to learn as much as possible. Second, you need marketing automation technology to facilitate appropriate communication delivery and to monitor and score interactive behavior. Third, you can gain a lot by interfacing with customers to validate the influence experienced by various stakeholders during their buying process. This can be achieved during the interview process for customer success stories if you've planned ahead to ask the right questions. This single conversation can help you develop the customer success story, a press release, details to flesh out personas, and fodder for use in content development from the customer's perspective.

You also must determine the best ways to establish a dialogue with an assortment of influencers. Sometimes it's just not possible to know exactly who in the organization needs to be educated prior to sales activities, so design your content to include additional resources that can be passed along by those you've already engaged. You empower them to be heroes by providing relevant information to the stakeholder who needs it—and you further your sales cause at the same time.

## CONVERSATIONS ACCELERATE NURTURING PROGRESSION

Virtual behavior has given marketing a host of interpretation points, but the personal touch adds a lot to building engagement and learning things you cannot "see" through online activities. Teleprospecting, whether outsourced or conducted by an inside sales team, is a valuable tool for progressing prospects through their buying journey.

I often work with Brian Carroll and his company, InTouch, to integrate eMarketing strategies with personalized telephone outreach. The combination enables higher-velocity progression and builds personalized engagement with prospects who are responsive to nurturing programs. Combining eMarketing with teleprospecting can produce results beyond eMarketing alone and helps to ensure that highly qualified buyers are transitioned to sales at the most opportune time.

### *Integrating Teleprospecting with Nurturing Programs: A Case Study*

A midsize IT solutions provider with a leading-company legacy for providing desktop management solutions had no trouble generating prospects. However, without a defined process for nurturing them, most of those prospects were ignored or lost over time. This situation originated because of a lack of agreement between marketing and sales as to the definition of a qualified prospect. Once the company firmly defined a qualified prospect, marketing was able to reengage existing prospects not sales ready and reengage older, dormant prospects sitting idle for at least six months.

The company employed a two-pronged approach that included a monthly e-mail campaign delivering thought-leadership content and telephone outreach. Personal calls were conducted at specific intervals to verify value delivered, offer additional relevant resources, and seek alignment with the qualified prospect specifications. The e-mails were sent from the same person assigned to call the prospects to create a more personalized sense of engagement.

The content used provided valuable information without ever mentioning the company's products by name. This was a very soft-messaging approach that relied on the sharing of expertise and strategic thinking to build engagement. Each successive content resource pulled the prospect farther into the company's expertise storyline and served to increase his desire to partner with a company that could effectively reduce the risk associated with solving the problem.

New prospects who entered the nurturing program began, with the first send, to build the story appropriately instead of their being added to that month's send list based on whenever they opted-in. The program has been underway for a year, and now uses 12 different nurturing e-mail sends each month, sent to prospects based on the time they entered the program.

The results are substantial:

- Marketing created a 200 percent increase in qualified prospects.
- The transition from prospect to sales opportunity increased 375 percent from 16 per month to 76 per month, on average.
- The company added $4.9 million in sales-pipeline growth in eight months.

This customer story provides proof that incorporating a human touch via strategic telephone outreach can add a substantial impact to your e-marketing outcomes. Accessing information digitally may be a preferred prospect activity at the start of the buying process, but there's no substitute for human contact to keep your prospects moving forward during a complex sale.

## BUYER EVOLUTION

If you haven't taken into account where and how your prospects and customers are finding and interacting with information as part of your eMarketing strategy–development process, you're missing a tremendous opportunity. The critical component of today's eMarketing strategy is pervasiveness. Your company and your contagious content must show up where your prospects spend their time on the Web. This is why broadening your scope to engage contacts beyond the decision maker needs to become a component you manage consistently.

In fact, in 2007, I attended the Tech Target Online ROI Summit and heard a CIO participating on a panel state that he relied on his staff to read and report back about their assessment of white papers, articles, and product research. He simply didn't have the time. He then added that his staff couldn't just report back; they had to sell him on the ideas to get him to begin to shift his perspective. How many of you are targeting marketing content to the staff that reports to decision makers? Evaluate that content to ensure that it's designed to help staff persuade the decision maker that the business value your company provides is worthy of his consideration.

Immersion into social media is changing how buyers research and find the products they purchase. If your content isn't where they are, your competitor's content most likely will be. Consider the example of a prospect who follows you on Twitter but is not a subscriber to the RSS feed from your blog. If you post a link to that blog post on Twitter, the prospect may click through and discover insights about a topic of interest that attracts her attention to your company. That prospect subsequently may come to rely on following your Twitter posts to know when additional items of relevance are posted to your blog or Web site. Making sure that you address prospect preferences for information discovery is critical.

As your content spreads and becomes more pervasive across the online channels where your prospects and customers spend their time, you create prospect interest. This means you have to keep on your toes and continue to deliver interesting, customer-centric content. The business landscape changes quickly, people get promoted, triggering events shuffle priorities—or even the identity of decision makers—and innovations shift mindsets. Your content must evolve along with your buyers to extend and further leverage the engagement you've begun.

*Chapter 15*

# Scoring for Prospect Progression

O ne of the really cool things about marketing automation technology is the ability to score engagement levels to help you see where prospects are in their buying process. A prospect's score also can help you learn their interests so that you can assign them to a relevant campaign or nurturing track. Only 5 to 15 percent of the prospects marketing generates are ready for sales conversations.[1] Lead scoring helps marketing to increase the quality of its presales interactions, pulling buyers farther through their buying process. Scoring also helps you to work with the sales team to define and agree on the actions that trigger a handoff.

Marketing's prospects need to be qualified from a sales perspective for sales to devote resources to pursue them. Scoring can help to solve this problem, but marketers have to recognize that scoring is more than assigning numbers to content and related prospect behavior. The trick is to make the numbers tell you what you need to know about that prospect.

When Pam Casale, CMO of Intellitactics, first developed a lead scoring method, her team arrived at the conclusion that a total score of 100 points equaled a sales opportunity. After implementing her new system, the inside sales team quickly learned that it was too late. Prospects had already begun conversations with competing vendors. Her team discovered that a lower score better reflected the sweet spot for sales success. Scoring is a constant work in progress. Your scoring methods need to evolve as you gain more insights into your prospects. Continuous refinement makes scoring pay off.

Scoring doesn't mean choosing a number, assigning points to content and behavior, and then transitioning prospects into the sales process when the number is reached. If you want scoring to contribute to the persistent progression of your prospects throughout their buying process, you have to be smart about it. You have to structure how new content will feed into the scoring process, at which buying stage, and how it plays into the story you're telling. Scoring activity will help to ensure you've routed the most relevant content to each potential buyer.

If your marketing automation system shows your prospects right on the edge of a conversion score, you need to have additional content planned to nudge them forward. Or you can plan for inside sales reps or telemarketing people to step in and make a personal connection and entice those prospects to move forward based on an offer tuned to their profile.

Finally, your scoring methodology should provide value to your sales team when the transition from prospect to sales opportunity takes place. Insights gathered during nurturing provide valuable information that salespeople can leverage to continue to move prospects forward with relevant conversations. Show salespeople which content prospects expressed interest in, and share any dialogue exchanged prior to the handoff. Scoring also depicts activities that held the highest interest and motivated responses. With knowledge derived from prospects' scores, salespeople are prepared to extend the relationships developed through marketing efforts.

## POINTS FOR CONTENT-DRIVEN INTERACTIONS

Marketing interaction depends on getting your prospects to respond to your content. You need to know which of your content is of interest to particular prospects and the corresponding behavior it motivates. Scoring prospect activity needs to focus on the reason for the interaction, not just the click. For example, a prospect accessing a variety of content that shows she is researching a foot-in-the door sale for your company should trigger a different marketing response than a prospect who appears to be randomly clicking. Both prospects may have the same numerical score, but their interest levels are likely quite different.

Content interactions can be scored progressively. Consider the following scenario: Your prospect receives a nurturing e-mail, clicks on the featured link, spends 3.23 minutes reading the article, clicks to download a white paper from a different area of your Web site, and leaves. The article was mapped to the midstage of the buyer's journey, but the white paper is tagged to a stage indicating a potential sales handoff. The time spent reading the article is past the 3 minutes it takes an average reader to digest that content. When you review the prospect's activity history, you see a trend of increasing time spent reading several content resources delivered during this nurturing campaign. The consistent evidence of increasing time spent across multiple related site resources is a more likely indication that the prospect actually was reading your content instead of having been interrupted or distracted while at your Web site.

You could miss a qualified prospect who doesn't fit the mold if your scoring methodology is focused solely on the prospect attaining a numerical score as a catalyst for sales activities. Beyond clicks, it's important to consider the context of the interactions.

### Content Scoring Options

**Content Theme**   A prospect is assigned to a nurturing track based on interest, which is expressed by his willingness to opt-in to access specific content. Proactively accessing additional related content beyond the e-mail link can be a prospect's way of showing you that he is moving faster through the buying process than your nurturing program. Scoring for the concentration of interactions the prospect takes in direct relation to that content theme helps you to gauge his degree of interest.

**Type of Sale**   When prospects interact heavily with content addressing topics related to a foot-in-the-door sale for your company, this can be an indication of a shorter time to purchase. In comparison, a solution that's typically an up-sell opportunity for an existing customer who has an established relationship with you may have a longer cycle.

**Buying-Process Stage**   Prospects need different types of information at different stages in their buying process. Since you've mapped your content to buying stages for each nurturing track, scoring access based on stage can indicate accelerating interest. For example, a prospect accessing content delivered via e-mail nurturing who starts proactively accessing ROI and total cost of ownership calculators may have just told you that she is creating a short list.

**Sales-Readiness Indicators**   Work closely with your sales team to determine specific content access known to be indicative of sales readiness. As you monitor prospects who become customers, you may see that a number of them viewed the online demo immediately before they entered into sales conversations. It's important to determine which of your content plays this role. By working with your sales force to determine which content is indicative of high interest, you can tie alerts to them to notify inside sales that it's time for a personal follow-up call.

**Keywords**   Keywords used as hyperlinks within articles can be used to indicate interest levels. By connecting the building blocks of your nurturing-track story, you invite the prospect to continue to learn more about a specific topic. In addition, the actual keywords prospects click on can provide insight into how they're searching for more information and what triggers a response. Specific keywords also can be indicative of buying stages.

**Related-Page Views**   Breaking online content articles into several pages and noting the differences between prospects who read two of four pages versus those who read all four pages of an article can tell you a great deal about depth of interest in that topic. If a majority of your prospects don't make it through the entire article, you may learn that it's missed the mark or that you delivered it at the wrong time in the buying process.

With targeted content scoring methods in place, you can create alerts to initiate specific actions tailored to the needs of your prospects instead of your scoring method. A nurturing track is designed to move prospects through the buying process. Prospects move at different paces. Creating triggers based on content-driven activity allows flexibility for managing and responding to them whenever the time is right.

eMarketing offers the power to learn about your prospects through their responses and interactions. If the only possible action they can take is to click to download your white paper, you've only given yourself the opportunity to learn one thing through that interaction. Include links within your white paper to draw them back to your

Web site for additional related information. With technology easing the difficulty of creating and publishing online content, keeping your prospects interactively engaged online is easier to facilitate. Gaining a better read on their interest levels and behavior helps marketing produce more sales-ready opportunities.

## MARKETO WALKS ITS TALK: A CASE STUDY

Jon Miller, vice president of marketing at marketing automation vendor Marketo, generously shared some insights about how his company "walked its talk" to generate over 130 customers in eight countries less than a year after its introduction in March 2008. Marketo structured its scoring efforts, aligned its marketing efforts with sales, and the business value is obvious.

Marketo embraced an iterative strategy when structuring its scoring methods. First, the company decided to attribute one point to each and every page at its Web site. Their Web-site visitors average 3.5 page views per visit. Then the company considered other factors such as keywords and content subject matter and applied some qualified "guesswork" to increase scores accordingly. Then it waited and watched for two months to gauge the outcomes and tweak the process.

The company involved its sales team from the start. As both marketing and sales watched and learned about the impact of the scoring strategy, they discovered keys that helped them to improve the process. First, they noticed that Web-site visitors who viewed the career page weren't likely to be prospects, so they discounted activity on that page. Second, they found that they needed to pay attention to both frequency and recency, diminishing scores over time for inactivity. When prospects reactivated their interest, the scores would increase appropriately.

The sales force confirmed that once a prospect's score reached a certain point, their calls were accepted more readily because the prospects actually knew who they were and could recall information they'd found valuable from Marketo. The company works continuously to improve alignment between marketing and sales. The two departments hold weekly meetings, review qualitative reports, and discuss improvements such as content timing, scoring, additional content needs, and overall focus. They also decided together to increase the points allotted for later-stage buying content.

Marketo has developed a 30-touch campaign with four different tracks based on roles. The company also lets its prospects choose whether they prefer the regular twice-per-month nurturing pace or the fast track with weekly communications. Then the company asks prospects for information incrementally, allowing prospects to trust the company before they are asked for more details and personal and professional data.

- The standard information collected when a prospect opts-in includes name, e-mail address, company, and title.
- During subsequent content downloads, prefilled forms ask for progressive information to fill out prospect profiles.
- Marketo also has developed a tiered qualification process to define the levels of engagement the company has established with its prospective customers.

The success of Marketo's nurturing programs speaks for itself:

- 1,500 new contacts (first tier) opt-in to nurturing each month. Thirty-three percent of those are "prospects," 25 percent of "prospects" are qualified as sales ready. The other 75 percent go into the nurturing program.
- Overall, 3.5 percent of those who opted-in to nurturing become sales-ready opportunities, yet certain behaviors indicate a much higher likelihood. For example, Marketo discovered a 9.5 percent conversion rate to sales-opportunity status for those who also visited the demo page on the company Web site.
- Marketo's sales team closes deals with 30 to 40 percent of the opportunities provided by marketing.
- Cold calls are a thing of the past.

Jon and his team weren't satisfied with just achieving these results. They decided to run some tests to determine the difference in progression between nurtured and nonnurtured contacts. The nurtured prospects showed a conversion-to-leads rate of 4 percent per month compared with 1 percent per month for those who received only the monthly newsletter. They learned that a total of 8 percent of nonnurtured prospects would become sales ready over the long term compared with 25 percent of those in nurturing programs.

No one can argue with the results that Marketo has achieved. It's important to note the iterative development of the company's eMarketing process and the alignment between marketing and sales. There's never been a better time to put an eMarketing strategy to work for your company.

## MICROSITES

Most corporate Web sites are focused on the company and display content based on product or service silos. Often, corporate Web sites act more as libraries of information than as active selling tools. Figure 15.1 shows the difference in context between a corporate Web site and a purposeful microsite landing page. Each is designed with a different purpose in mind.

When compared with corporate Web sites, microsites can be designed around a number of eMarketing themes. Potential themes include a market segment, a problem-to-solution journey, or an industry educational portal. The technology is now business-user friendly for content publishing, and the cost is low enough to enable many companies to deploy as many as they need, complete with demand-generation and nurturing tools.

Microsites are easier to update and control. They give marketers the flexibility they need to respond quickly to market changes and gain better insights when scoring prospect behavior. By pulling your prospects to a rich content experience designed to help them solve a high-priority issue, you've created the opportunity to find out just how interested they are in solving that problem. Note that the content links on the right side of the microsite in the figure include education, evidence, and expertise content options related to the problem-to-solution theme.

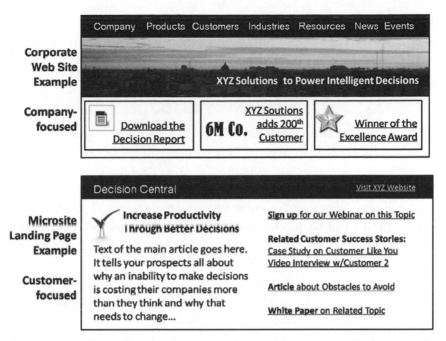

**Figure 15.1**    The difference in context between a corporate Web site and a purposeful microsite.

With a marketing automation system behind the scenes of your microsite, you have the tools to help you focus exclusively on building engagement that drives buying decisions. Each additional content resource added to the microsite helps to build the story designed around your prospect's needs. Information in the sidebar can be updated and reorganized easily based on prospect behavioral insights. Keyword hyperlinks can be tested and adjusted to coincide with prospect interests. Managing your marketing content to coordinate with prospect needs can happen in real time. And when prospects click on the link to the corporate Web site, their action may indicate a shift to active buying intention.

Every company wants sizzling hot opportunities. Those are the ones your sales team drops everything to pursue. For marketing to generate these sought-after hot prospects, you've got to know more than interest levels. Your eMarketing strategies need to also score behavioral triggers. These triggers help you to deliver even more personalized content and innovative solution ideas to turn engagement into action at the transition to sales.

## e-MAIL NEWSLETTERS

Marketers state that e-mail newsletters are the most effective online medium for lead generation and nurturing—ahead of both customer success stories and white papers.[2] Most corporate Web sites have a newsletter subscription offer displayed prominently. A newsletter generally includes a mix of company information, articles, a featured sales offer or call to action, upcoming events, and product releases. Newsletters are a way to stay in touch and are usually sent monthly to the company's subscriber list.

Content publishing tools and e-mail service providers have made it easier for marketers to produce and send these communications with the goals of driving Web traffic and distributing content. The advent of marketing automation tools enables marketers to increase their visibility into subscriber behavior, increasing the value of newsletters as a scoring tool that helps to determine interests and assign nurturing tracks.

Where a nurturing e-mail program will include one call to action, a newsletter format enables marketers to use multiple. Marketers can combine the types of information and topics showcased in a newsletter to enable subscribers to "vote" on what they're interested in learning more about. Instead of using your newsletter as a general "keep in touch" medium, consider the advantages to be gained by using it strategically.

### Three Strategic Tips for E-Newsletters

1. General newsletters should be used to determine priority interests. For example, let's say that your products solve three different problems. Feature content articles on each of those problem topics. Subscribers who repeatedly respond (e.g., two or three times) to a specific topic, ignoring the others, can be sent an e-mail offering them the option to receive more related information based

on that problem-to-solution scenario. When they opt-in, they've just self-selected a nurturing track, telling you that the topic is important to them. Score this interactive exchange as a progressive step.

2. Sidebar information about company events, product releases, and other information should be positioned in your newsletters to tell you something important when a subscriber responds. If a subscriber responds predominantly to sidebar content, consider what he could be telling you about his buying stage or interests. For example, if a sidebar link is related to a new feature release a customer is using, the prospect may be telling you about a new initiative you can help him achieve. Or if a prospect clicks on a link promoting a Webinar, check the topic against other content the prospect has accessed recently. This could indicate a shift forward in the prospect's buying process.

3. Sending your newsletter to different market segments with corresponding content enables you to increase the relevance for your prospects. This doesn't mean using totally different content. It simply could involve changing the wording of titles and summaries and the sidebar selections. For example, a Webinar offered to one segment might be switched out for a white paper with more relevance to another segment.

E-newsletters are a terrific vehicle for lead generation and prospect profiling. When you target newsletters to specific audiences, you increase the value they receive and the quality of information you can gather—and they become nurturing media as well. Consider that a customer newsletter also should be targeted appropriately. Your customers need a different level of information from prospects. Scoring customer behavior based on newsletter content designed to help them extend the use of your product offerings to increase value helps marketers to determine when an up-sell or cross-sell opportunity arises.

## PROGRESSING PROSPECTS TO SALES

Recent research shows that 52 percent of B2B companies do not screen the quality of the prospects they pass on to sales.[3] This includes prospects whose data consists only of contact information, such as business cards gathered at a trade show, for example, plus all the other inbound responses to marketing initiatives. Additionally, 56 percent of companies admit that they lack a formal lead-nurturing process.[4] Employing the right eMarketing strategy changes all this and focuses marketing on nurturing progressing prospects to qualified sales readiness.

Marketing must quantify its contribution to its company's bottom line. The right content and nurturing approach will prove that marketing is providing valuable contributions that help salespeople to increase win rates, as well as shorten time to revenue. The only way to truly and consistently create the flow of prospects from marketing to sales is to involve sales in the determination of when a prospect becomes an opportunity.

Use the four structured alignment points listed below to shape the marketing-to-sales process. Each point will increase your ability to keep sales moving forward in synch with prospect needs. The closer marketing and sales work together in defining the meaning of prospect activity, the more invested both become in ensuring their interactions with prospects are refined continuously and tuned for optimal results.

### Four Marketing-to-Sales Alignment Points

1. Make sure that sales and marketing agree on the definition of a qualified prospect. Get specific, and make a list of attributes that can be gathered and proven by marketing during the nurturing process. Take the discussion beyond demographics to encompass buyer scenarios, foot-in-the-door sales indicators, and industry trends that cause priority shifts.

2. Enlist the help of sales to determine which content interactions indicate deeper stages of the buying process. Decide if there are prerequisite activities that lead to this point, and make sure to use them. For example, a salesperson confirms that requesting a personalized demo is the key indicator for sales readiness. If marketing focuses only on getting that outcome and jumps past foundational buying stages, the quality of the prospects as

potential buyers could be undercut. Prospects may need more education to fully appreciate the demo. It's important to honor the buying process your prospects prefer while understanding which triggers are the important ones to act on.

It's also helpful to consider whether or not that conversion touch point needs to shift when applied to prospects in different roles or industries. The same behavior by different individuals isn't necessarily indicative of the same intention.

3. Identify the top five things sales needs to know about each prospect to step seamlessly into the relationship. Develop a plan for how to gather those insights consistently by incorporating them into your eMarketing strategy. An example might be in asking progressive form questions for each substantial download of content as the relationship with a prospect develops. A priority for sales also could include providing the sales rep with a summary of a prospect's activity history to date or knowing which content a prospect accessed when her access frequency increased right before the handoff. Make sure these are the things salespeople agree they need to move forward, not what marketing thinks the sales rep should have.

4. Prepare three or four qualifying questions (and the desired answers) for inside sales or teleprospecting to use to help gauge when a prospect is becoming sales ready. These questions could include authority, timeline, and budget, but they also may include the objective the prospect is trying to obtain and the problem description from the prospect's perspective. Be creative and reach beyond factual yes or no questions to glean insights that position the salesperson to create relevant buyer focused conversations.

Alignment efforts between sales and marketing improve the outcomes for both departments. Recent research by Aberdeen Group found that the two top pressures on sales and marketing were to increase top-line revenues (56 percent) and increase sales productivity (60 percent).[5] When marketing and sales work together to enable the graceful progression of prospects through their buying process, the result is shortened time to revenue.

Chapter 16

# Alignment Accelerates Progression

M arketing and sales tend to operate independently even though they work two ends of what should be a seamless process. When the two departments work together, they have the opportunity to power increased revenues and profits. Collaborating to develop and agree on a unified eMarketing strategy that covers the entire buying process will align their efforts productively. Each side has insights, information, and processes that affect the other. Some impacts are more demonstrable than others, but if your marketing-to-sales process is in synch, the impact will be obvious.

Consider that 70 percent of companies interviewed said that sales reps spend fewer than one and a half days a week speaking with clients or prospects, not including preparation time, travel time, or voice mail/e-mail. And of those, 30 percent said their sales reps spend *less than a day per week* speaking with clients or prospects.[1] Based on its sales enablement research, IDC concludes, "In short, [sales reps] spend a third of their potential selling time in sales preparation activities that could be done better by automated systems and improved processes."[2] Effective eMarketing strategies must reach farther into the pipeline than ever before to enable salespeople to focus on selling. Marketing needs to work with sales to help create greater sales efficiencies that produce more revenue opportunities.

When marketing and sales are aligned, feedback channels are opened to allow continuous bidirectional communications. Sales needs support on a daily basis, and marketing needs insights fresh from the street, as close to real time as possible. When marketers gain information from salespeople to enable a needed revision to a nurturing article right away, effectiveness in prospect engagement improves in step with marketing efforts. Similarly, if salespeople have sales content they can use easily, time spent not selling is eliminated. Instead, the salespeople are out on the street gathering intelligence from face-to-face interactions that can be used to make marketing even more relevant.

Marketing is in the perfect position to enable sales to spend more time selling by taking the initiative to provide salespeople with information, content, and prospect intelligence that serves to reduce nonselling time. In addition, sales content that's aligned with marketing efforts and buyer synopses serves to help improve win rates and selling efficiencies. Marketing stands to reap huge benefits, including improved impact on revenue generation, higher engagement for marketing programs, and influence on shortening sales cycles, by aligning with sales.

## THE HANDOFF AND THE TAKE-BACK

Marketing is being given an executive mandate to provide the sales force with opportunities and prove business-value contribution. To answer this challenge successfully, marketing can better facilitate the transition of sales-ready prospects to the sales force by creating a standardized handoff process. A well-designed transition provides salespeople with a seamless entry to the prospect relationship.

The best transitions happen when marketing provides the information sales needs to get into the conversation effectively. The appropriate content and the context around a prospect's interactions with the company gives sales a roadmap for his progress to date. With a standardized handoff process, marketing can offer salespeople the tools they need to enter the conversation in step with the needs of the prospect.

This sales kit might include the following:

- A definition of the triggering event that caused the handoff
- An activity record for the prospect during nurturing programs, including the timing and frequency of interactions
- A summary of content viewed/downloaded with a suggested set of relevant sales collateral. A sales collateral kit might include

  - A problem-to-solution brief based on the prospect's interest indications

  - An industry review and notes about the latest trends that could impact the prospect's business

  - A customer success story—same problem, industry, and size, if possible

  - Selected slides the salesperson can use to create a personalized presentation relevant to that prospect

Everything in this sales kit is or should be accessible to marketing and sales. The sales kit should be organized around the way prospects buy, not the way your internal culture is oriented—by product lines or industries, for example. Marketing automation systems provide activity histories, and the rest should be made available by your sales portal—creating a process that is understood and agreed on by salespeople. Spend time training them on the use of the tools and the meaning and context behind personas representative of prospect actions.

The process you create needs to include a way for marketing to take back prospects who prove to be longer term. Whether or not sales closes a deal, feedback is critical. Salespeople should be able to recommend a focus for further nurturing activity based on their contact with the prospect.

By mining direct sales experiences, you can learn a lot about what's working and what's not. Learning about new problems along with which content prospects find valuable and then confirming the actual buying stage of prospects at the handoff can continuously help in reassessing and refining nurturing programs to improve progression over time.

## INFLUENCERS AND DETRACTORS

Most B2B complex sales involve solutions that have an impact on the company beyond the project team. Politics within organizations vary, and often heavy influence can be wielded by people or situations outside both marketing and sales visibility. Influencers can include friends, peers, colleagues, industry experts, analysts, subconscious preferences, and even the confidence level of your prospects themselves.

From the opposite spectrum, detractors can include everything from competitors to objection handling, word choices, misinterpretations, peers with other vendor recommendations, and negative press coverage. Even a discussion posted on LinkedIn with comments that vary from what your prospect believes to be true about your product can detract from your ability to progress the prospect through the buying process.

One of the best ways to support influencers and minimize detractors is to tell each of them a consistent story across all touch points. People who influence the purchase decision have differing agendas. Marketers and sales reps interact with a number of influencers throughout their relationship with a prospect company. Combining information gathered virtually by marketing with personal interactions experienced by salespeople helps both sides to learn more about what's important to each type of influencer.

Influencers and detractors don't care whether they're interacting with marketing or with salespeople. In fact, they may not even make a distinction between the two. Each of them cares about what's important to him. Learning how to best address these needs will help marketing and sales add value to influencers and minimize or circumvent the impact of detractors—in some cases even persuading them to change their view. With firm alignment, interruptions to the fluidity of the buying experience can be addressed appropriately.

## INCORPORATING INSIGHTS

The only way that insights gained from prospect and customer interactions have impact is if they're incorporated into your eMarketing strategies. If salespeople take their time to provide marketing with insights, they want to see that information put to use. Once they see the impact their feedback has on prospect quality and helpful sales tools that shorten time to sales, they'll start looking for other ways they can contribute. Likewise, if marketing takes on the effort to use that feedback to modify personas and produce both content and information for the sales team, sales reps need to hold up their end of the deal. Proof that closing the loop has a positive impact on the results marketing and sales achieve will help to make this loop self-perpetuating.

Closed-loop feedback should be used to address a variety of issues, including the reasons for a sales lead that becomes a longer-term opportunity, why sales wins a deal, and what further tools and collateral salespeople need to increase their ability to win more deals. By creating a targeted focus for each feedback purpose, the information sales provides to marketing can be applied easily to optimize joint efforts.

### Feedback about Prospects Returned to Nurturing

The most efficient method for taking a prospect back into nurturing is to design an evaluation process the salesperson can complete quickly to help marketing improve prospect quality over time. Limit this to the most important five to seven points that will help in the development of a qualified sales opportunity. Getting this feedback is critical, so you need to involve sales in the design of the evaluation to ensure that salespeople buy into the process. The best way to collect this feedback is via an online survey. It's even better if the results also can be archived with the prospect's data.

---

Although the sales evaluation questions should be tailored specifically to your company, some possible inclusions for the returned prospect include

- A dropdown selection of reasons the prospect is being returned: "Not short term," "Unable to qualify as opportunity," "No budget allocation," "Not ready to talk," etc.
- Which buying stage is the prospect in?
- An indicator for which campaign the prospect should be assigned to for further nurturing.
- A date for a requalifying interaction ("Call in six months").
- A text box for insights the salesperson learned about the prospect and her company.
- A selector indicating the problem the prospect is trying to answer. Include an "Other" choice with a text field in case the prospect's perspective is different from the choices you know about.
- A rating of the quality level of the prospect (from 1 to 10).

---

Compiling these results into monthly or quarterly scorecards can help marketing to benchmark its progress at closing the gap between the quality of the prospects its hands off to sales and those that sales clamors to receive.

### Feedback about Customer Wins

When the end result is a won deal, a feedback survey should be designed to help marketers produce more opportunities like that one.

Make sure the answers are archived with the customer record because they also can be incorporated into a future customer success story.

Some ideas for evaluation questions and follow-up for a win survey might include

- Indicate the top three reasons the customer chose our company.
- What problem is the customer solving with our solution?
- Which product(s) or solution did the customer purchase?
- Which of the following sales collateral did you use?
- Assign the new customer to a customer nurturing program.
- How many people who you know about were involved in the decision process?
- Which competitors did the customer evaluate during the buying process?
- Which content and information did the customer find most relevant?
- How many interactions did the salesperson have before the deal closed?
- How many days did the prospect spend in sales activities after hand-off?

It's wise to work with salespeople to define dropdown answer terminology for the questions so that it matches how they think. The easier you can make it for sales to use the win evaluation survey intuitively, the more likely they'll be to complete it with solid information that marketers can use.

### Feedback for Sales Enablement

Marketing also needs feedback from sales to provide better content and collateral that salespeople actually will use during sales activities. With this information, marketing can enable sales to continue the story they've started and continue advancing prospects toward purchase.

The following seven pointers will help you begin to develop a strategic plan for improved alignment by collecting valuable information marketing can put to work to better support the sales process:

1. Learn the sales process from preconversation through customer acquisition so that marketing can anticipate and develop materials for the ways salespeople will use them.
2. Find out how salespeople prepare and research to enter a sales conversation, and determine what exists in marketing that will help them to streamline the process.
3. Assess how salespeople are using the marketing content you already provide—or why they aren't. Remove any content they're not using so it doesn't get in the way.
4. Ask salespeople what information they really need but don't have easy access to, and determine the best way to provide it.
5. Categorize insights to address buyer scenarios. Incorporate them into your personas, and provide updated versions to your sales team.
6. Discover what salespeople do to personalize the content, collateral, and presentations they use during sales activities. Redesign that information to make it easier to use.
7. Learn what your competitors are saying about your products and company, and prepare conversational briefs to help salespeople alleviate prospect concerns.

## CREATE A USEFUL SALES PORTAL

Most sales portals serve as an archive for marketing materials. Your sales portal needs to be a productive workspace for your sales force. As such, it needs to be organized around the tracks and approaches that define your buyers. It also needs to be presented in a way that streamlines access to what your salespeople need to engage those buyers. When you employ the seven pointers in the last section, you'll know how to structure sales portal information to improve and streamline the way sales accesses, compiles, and uses the knowledge that marketing provides. The objective should be to enable your salespeople to get a complete overview quickly that helps them to pursue a specific sales opportunity. Combined with the prospect information your marketing automation system delivers, the sales portal should provide the tools your salespeople need to keep buyers progressing toward purchase.

So let's put the sales portal in context. Depending on your company's unique attributes, information should be grouped in a contextual arrangement on your sales portal. The sales process is an extension of the marketing process. Your sales portal should serve to share the marketing side and incorporate it with the sales side. When content display is structured to give sales reps a comprehensive grasp of prospects' experience to date, as well as knowledge of how to initiate and extend the sales conversation with target prospect segments, they have exactly what they need to focus on selling.

Including the following four types of content on your sales portal can help to streamline the time it takes for salespeople to prepare for sales activities.

### Problem-to-Solution Scenarios

Marketing is leveraging problem-to-solution scenarios to generate prospect engagement. Since these scenarios depict the buying process from start to finish, using them as the basis for content arrangement on your sales portal helps sales to align easily with buyers' needs. Although you'll want to include access to related marketing content, the sales portal should focus on sales content created to extend the storyline. Include a scenario brief that outlines the story across the buying process so that salespeople can easily determine where they're entering the relationship when they review a prospect's activity history.

### Personas or Buyer Synopses

Depending on how sophisticated your segmentation strategies are, you may be employing full-blown personas and buyer synopses that salespeople can use to familiarize themselves quickly as they develop presentation and conversational strategies with higher impact. Regardless of how you're defining and segmenting your prospects during nurturing, that information needs to be shared with your sales team. Including relevant terminology and talking points for each persona or segment type also provides salespeople with fodder for both conversational exchanges and written communications used to advance buyers effectively.

### Industry Profiles

Most companies market to at least several industries. Different nuances, terminology, and expertise are involved in selling to each one. It's not enough to know how to help your prospect solve a problem. Buyers expect salespeople to know their business and their current market environment. The problems, compliance regulations, and competitive pressures companies in one industry face may be off the radar or inapplicable to another.

The more up-to-date information about the industry that marketing can provide to sales, the easier it is for sales to prepare for conversational activities. It's worth noting that if marketing is developing consistent and targeted content for specific segments, they are already doing this research. Including links to useful articles on industry community Web sites also can provide sales reps with a helpful way to share valuable information focused on helping their prospects gain insights into the problems they're trying to solve. And don't forget to include trend and forward-looking data.

Prospects are interested in the future, as well as the present. Most of them would rather create a relationship with a vendor for the long term than be faced with another vendor evaluation when a project requiring similar expertise comes along.

### Competitive Differentiation

Unless your company is way over the edge on innovation, it's unlikely that you don't have competition for customers. In order for marketing to develop content that differentiates your company from others, it likely also has created a competitive matrix or strengths, weaknesses, opportunities, and threats (SWOT) analysis. For your sales team, provide the matrix and include talking points next to each item to help your salespeople respond easily without seeming defensive if buyers raise these points. Conversational redirects that help to refocus the customer on value are helpful. After all, your product is the best choice for solving your prospect's problems, right?

A useful sales portal ensures that salespeople are primed for conversations in synch with the opportunities they're working on closing. Figure 16.1 shows one way to create a contextual display of information for a sales portal built around a problem-to-solution scenario.

| Problem X: | Solution to X: | Buyer Information: |
|---|---|---|
| Scenario brief outlining the story: Include causes and industry trends for target markets. | Expertise content about how product solves problem. | Personas/Profiles Buyer Synopses |
| | Customer Successes | Sales Feedback |
| Impact if not solved | Analyst Reports White Papers | Industry Information Vertical 1 |
| Competitors' Spiel | Build a Presentation | **Marketing:** Qualified Lead Defn. |
| Buyer 's Obstacles to solving the problem | Company Experts | Current related campaigns & content |
| | Sales & Solution | |
| Conversational Collateral ,Messaging | Collateral & Messaging | Transitional Content for the shift to sales. |

**Figure 16.1** Sales portal relevance.

Information about the problem the prospect is facing is displayed in the left column. Solution content is displayed down the middle, and marketing context is supplied on the right. This snapshot is oriented for one industry trying to solve one problem.

Marketing should have analytics enabled on the sales portal to track who uses which content, what is most popular, and which content is clearly missing the mark in usefulness for your sales team. Tying those statistics to sales wins and benchmarking cycle time from the marketing handoff can provide solid validation for how well marketing is supporting sales.

In addition to the salesperson feedback surveys, enabling comments and ratings for sales portal content can help marketing to evolve sales content continuously, as well as collect tribal knowledge that can be shared across the sales team. Developing a process that enables marketing to continuously provide sales reps with content they'll not only use but also find instrumental in closing deals is the key.

## END-GAME STAMINA

Maybe marketers are focusing too much on volume. Smaller, more controllable, personalized, and in-depth buyer handoffs may be the best way to begin to impact sales results. Once marketing has perfected the development of qualified prospects salespeople can close, then it can scale the process to increase volume. When marketing becomes known as a provider of opportunities, salespeople will stop spending their time generating their own leads and start relying on marketing-produced prospects—because they buy.

With a consistent flow of valid opportunities each month, pretty soon sales has a pipeline that makes a difference to revenue outcomes—instead of more prospect volume of questionable quality. What it comes down to is incremental change vetted and tuned at each step with successes that increase alignment between marketing and sales.

One of the biggest issues facing marketing is maintaining end-game stamina. Because sales is focused on short-term outcomes, marketing responds by trying to move faster at creating a volume of opportunities for sales to pursue. But you can't push prospects beyond where they're ready to be. Prospects don't give one whit about your company's quarterly quotas or the demand in your sales pipeline. When marketing can't gain momentum effectively, it tends to turn to short-term lead-generation tactics and drop longer-term targeted nurturing strategies. Longer-term prospects are relegated to a general "keep in touch" campaign that can cease to motivate them farther in their consideration process.

Motivating a prospect to take the next step in her purchase process can take from five to nine contacts or more depending on the prospect's stage in the buying process. If marketing pursues a three-month campaign and makes three contacts and then quits, it has given up too soon. Marketing has invested dollars in generating and cultivating that prospect, and it needs to make that investment pay off. Starting over with a fresh idea has the potential of diminishing prospect interest if it's outside the storyline that the prospect embraced from the start. Likewise, when marketing supports sales reps during step-backs with the talking points and knowledge they need to move prospects forward in the buying journey, sales will be empowered to get that deal back on track.

## Chapter 17

# Stories that Progress Sales Conversations

To achieve persistent progression, eMarketing strategies need to have an impact on the buying process from status quo to choice. This is done initially through fresh, relevant, and enticing demand-generation programs to engage prospects, followed by natural-nurturing interactions that deliver valuable information and move the process along. As engagement is built over time, prospects are transformed into qualified sales opportunities. Ideally, marketers smoothly transition the buyer relationship to the sales force and continue working to enable the salesperson to turn that buyer into a customer.

The sales team is responsible for validating what the prospect has been lead to believe. Your prospect's confidence and comfort level can diminish unless the salesperson reinforces the prospect's current perceptions and provides added value. In order to align the sales process with the marketing experience, your eMarketing strategy needs to reach beyond the transition point to develop content, communications, and collateral that help salespeople get the buyer to take the last steps in choosing to become your customer.

This objective can be achieved when marketing becomes the steward of your company's conversational and buyer knowledge. Marketers need to gather and leverage that intelligence effectively to create an ongoing story that invites participation, enables buyers to visualize success, and helps salespeople consistently win deals. The secret is continuous and compelling customer focus in execution.

The best way to help your salespeople do this is by leveraging the storyline you developed for your eMarketing strategy. Your storyline is the consistent thread throughout your marketing-to-sales programs and is based on your customers' needs, concerns, and most urgent priorities. Stories are visual. They're contagious. They spread among influencers to decision makers to colleagues and peers. They have pass-along word-of-mouth (WOM) value. A salesperson who shows up to talk about your company without demonstrating knowledge about the buyer's business and extending the strategic ideas planted by marketing will find it difficult to have a meaningful conversation. Extending the storyline your prospect has engaged with into sales conversations enhances results.

## CONVERSATIONAL GAMBITS

The term *gambit* in old marketing meant making a move to gain an advantage. In attraction marketing, *gambit* means to take an action to open a conversation. In a digital business environment where buyers have taken control of their buying journey, the process must shift from chasing your buyers to enticing them to seek you out. The marketing-to-sales process best interfaces with the buying process when it's designed around a holistic engagement strategy.

When marketing is focused on matching its communications and content to prospect interests, the interactive dialogue established with people is different. It's focused on growing engagement through value exchange. Therefore, when the handoff of an opportunity to sales occurs, that salesperson needs to have conversational resources at the ready. The old feeds-and-speeds focused-pitch conversations will not endear your salespeople to your prospective customers. In fact, if marketing has focused on prospects' needs throughout the buying process, this approach will be off-putting and diminish the value marketing has established with all its prior efforts. In other words, this disconnect is wasting marketing investments.

To counter this disconnect, marketers can provide salespeople with conversational gambits they can use to step into the dialogue at the time of handoff. By setting up conversation starters related to the marketing content the prospect has viewed, salespeople will be ready to pick up the dialogue. At the time of content development, marketing can streamline effort by creating sales resources at the same time and with the same research undertaken to create buyer synopses and develop content.

Providing sales with customer-focused conversational resources is extremely important, given your buyers' access to extensive information. Buyers already know a lot about your products by the time they talk to your salesperson. But problems and solutions have grown in complexity. Evaluating the options available to remove obstacles to business success is not an easy process. More people are involved—more moving parts, more considerations, and ultimately, more risk. Buyers want salespeople who can come into the conversation with strategic ideas that demonstrate they understand the buyer's business needs as well as his concerns—this means everyone in the group, not just one decision maker. Marketing can provide materials to help salespeople evolve these conversations.

The best way to create a library of relevant conversational gambits is to have marketing take the lead. In addition to drawing from content, conversational gambits can be cultivated from customer feedback, responses to interactive marketing, social networking observations and exchanges, blog comments, and salespeople's experiences. Once you're using customer-focused content combined with natural nurturing, it makes good business sense to set up the hand-off of sales-ready prospects with easily assimilated marketing story extensions.

Consider creating a way to aggregate all these informational inputs, and then organize them by problem-solution scenarios, personas, or industries—whatever method matches how you're segmenting your eMarketing programs. This helps with continuity, as well as context and focus.

To make the idea of conversational gambits easier to envision, think about what happens when you facilitate an introduction between two people you know. What do you do? Well, usually, you give each of them a bit of background information on the other. Then you talk about why you're introducing the two of them—usually related to a common interest or objective.

> Sally, meet John. He's the best source for information on widgets that I know. In fact, he helped ABC Company create that campaign that went viral last year.

> John, meet Sally. Sally is looking for ideas on how to integrate a widget into her company's demand-generation process.

This is similar to how marketers should consider introducing salespeople to buyers. By facilitating an introductory conversation, you'll set your salesperson off on the right foot. The introduction works best when it extends both ways. In other words, it needs to happen both for the salesperson and for the prospect. Consider how an introduction can extend the story you've been unfolding for your prospect during nurturing.

Sally, I'd like to introduce you to John. He's an expert at helping companies think about and evaluate the available options for optimizing power use in data centers. He's worked with a number of larger research facilities like yours and can share some examples with you about how they not only reduced cooling costs but also maximized their use of space.

John, I'd like to introduce you to Sally. Sally works for ABC Research facility in Austin, and she recently read our white paper, "Green Solutions that Reduce Cooling Costs in Data Centers." She'd like to know how . . .."

How many times have you ever received an introduction like this at the time of handoff to a salesperson? Not only does it set up both sides for a meaningful conversation, but it's also good business etiquette. It's considerate of both parties, and it humanizes the relationship. And it's the type of practice respected colleagues participate in with each other every day. An introduction like this not only tells Sally that you've "heard" her request and validated it by matching her up with an expert prepared to help her, but it also sets up John (your salesperson) for the conversation. He's got a jump-start on preparing for this conversation because he knows exactly how to pick up the dialogue. It's smooth and keeps everyone in his comfort zone, at the same time encouraging the buyer to take the next step in the buying journey.

Now extend this thinking. Conversational gambits are not just for introductions at handoff. Think about the remaining stages of the buying journey and how you can help salespeople to create conversations during each of them. When your salespeople are set up to follow a conversational flow, they will be less likely to falter in their attempt to grow that relationship into a customer.

## CUSTOMERS LIKE THEM

Customer referrals and reviews are the most trusted forms of marketing content for business-to-consumer sales. This is due to people putting more trust in people they consider more like them than anyone else. Considering that B2B prospects also are consumers, stories about people like them solving similar problems will be more engaging than company postulations. The problem salespeople have is not that they don't know your customers' stories but rather that they don't articulate them in ways that help buyers visualize how the solution applies to their specific situations. Buyers are pressed for time. They don't have the latitude to spend a lot of it trying to determine how your offering will provide the outcome they want. Using customer stories conversationally means getting beyond the product specs and flat statistics and helping buyers weave their own stories to equate the benefits.

Since marketing already has transformed all of your dry, product-focused case studies into customer success stories, providing sales with conversational examples related to your company's target segments is easier than you may think. In order to provide salespeople with a customers-like-them story strategy, go back to the cutting-room floor and look at what you left out of your public versions of these success stories. Review the customer interviews you did to produce them, and talk to the salespeople who sold those customers. Create small conversational pieces that include industry insights to help your salespeople show prospects that they understand their business. Orient these content resources around problem-to-solution scenarios to keep them customer-focused.

Consider creating expanded versions of customer success stories that salespeople can send after a great conversation with a buyer to extend her understanding of how another company like hers solved a similar problem. By including information that's not freely available on your corporate Web site but of high interest and relevance, your salesperson will add value to what that buyer already knows about your company and customers. The salesperson can become instrumental in bringing clarity to the buyer's decision.

To set yourself up for the variety of ways you can apply customer success stories to the buying process, make sure to interview influencers and other stakeholders who were affected by the successful project implementation and outcome. Providing insights that help buyers to persuade all a project's stakeholders in your favor can help you to move the buyer progressively toward choice. And it can help you to set up conversational scenarios that your salespeople may encounter with the different influencers themselves.

By ensuring that your customers-like-them stories are oriented for conversational extensions, marketing is helping sales use those examples in meetings and phone conversations. Those stories also help establish conversations within the buyers' organization between and among the people who influence the final purchase decision.

## ATTAINABLE OBJECTIVES

Selling complex solution offerings involves multiple interactions after the prospect is handed off from marketing to sales. With each step, the salesperson should have an objective that's attainable. This does not mean to close the deal. Attainable objectives are steps along the buyer's process that move the buyer closer to a purchase decision. The reality companies need to account for is that buyers very rarely move down a predictable, linear path to choice.

To get started, marketing needs to learn from salespeople which goals they have with each sales activity. Just as all marketing content should have a call to action, the stories that marketing creates for use by sales must have an attainable objective. For example; if the goal is to find out who the influencers are, seed your sales rep with a story that invites the buyer to respond with that information, perhaps even an introduction so that your sales rep can tell the story directly.

Perhaps the goal is to find out which competitors are also being considered or even what they're saying about your company. What story can you tell that differentiates your company and product offerings from the competition? What underlying goal wasn't articulated at the beginning of an existing customer's project that you helped solve during the implementation? Answers to questions such as these can help in the development of compelling sales stories.

It's important to note that attainable objectives swing both ways. Just as your salespeople need to be armed with stories that help them to take the next step, these stories also need to help buyers' meet their objectives. It cannot be said enough that the better you know your customers, the better you'll be at creating stories that help both sides attain their objectives from each sales interaction.

## PRESENTATIONS WITH PUNCH

Presentations are both a marketing tool and a sales tool. The most common use for marketing initiatives is Webinars. The most common use for salespeople is buyer meetings. PowerPoint is a wonderful tool that somehow became most used as a type of public script. Slides so full of text, bullet points, and miniscule charts no one can understand or decipher are the norm. And they're boring. Creating this type of presentation is a sure sign of laziness.

Presentations are meant to be a backdrop for the words and ideas of the speaker. They're meant to add flavor and texture, not serve as a teleprompt. There are some great books on how to create compelling presentations, so I'll leave that subject to those experts. Ultimately, presentations that keep people interested in the ideas being expressed and invite dialogue are what salespeople need—and marketers are in a great position to help them out.

The secret to presentations with punch is that they're all about the audience. And, for a sales conversation, the focus needs to be on solving a problem or answering a need the prospective buyer has. Because marketing has access to the activity history of the prospects, has designed personas, written content to address identified interests, and interviewed customers like the prospects for success stories, it has already laid the foundation for terrific presentations.

When creating a presentation, the salesperson needs to think about it as telling a story. There's no earthly way to tell a compelling story if the slides your salespeople have to choose from are all about your company. How many times have you been in a presentation where the first slide is about the company's value proposition? This is followed by the company history and then that awful slide full of client logos, which is like looking at an out-of-focus kaleidoscope. Trust me, if you're invited to present to a prospective buyer, he already has seen all this stuff on your Web site. And the people who haven't don't care. They care about getting their needs answered in the best possible way. They're interested in seeing if you can prove that your company delivers on the promises marketing has already made.

Presentations created as follow-on to previous marketing story exposure means that marketers can set up salespeople to extend that story seamlessly. Below are several ideas for how to equip your sales team with all the components they need to create presentations with punch.

### Solution-Story Slides

Consider creating minidecks that have five to seven slides focused on addressing a specific problem/solution scenario. If your product has a lot of features, create a slide for each one so that salespeople can select only the information that's pertinent to a specific opportunity. Less definitely can be more. Attention wavers when people are exposed to too much information or if that information strays from the main issue at hand. If the presentation story is told well, the buying committee will ask questions that enable the sales rep to expand the conversation in a way that increases value instead of rambling on about things the buyers don't care about.

### Validation Slides

Create slide decks by industry, customer size, or however your customer segments break down. People want to know how other companies solve similar problems and see the successful outcomes you've helped them achieve. Do these in sets of four:

1. Establish the problem.
2. Highlight reasons the customer chose your product offering.
3. Show how your product was incorporated into the existing company infrastructure.
4. Expose the resulting business value.

### Company Slides

Yes, you'll need a few—at the end. Use no more than two or three. Think about how you can design company slides that have impact and create interest. Instead of the boring usual company slides, create a slide that showcases customer benefits that add value to the relationship. Showcase your customers' community forum, expertise blog, and direct and immediate contact with support personnel. If you participate in charitable activities, create a slide about social participation. In other words, focus your company slides on what your company delivers to your customers that they would otherwise not receive or perhaps are even unaware exists. In this way, even though you're talking about your company, you're still talking about the value you deliver to your customers.

Marketing has the information and the insight to background material to create compelling slide decks that salespeople can use to tell stories instead of reciting a litany of boring facts and statistics out of context. In addition to creating the slide deck, give salespeople pointers in the notes area for each slide. In this way, if they select and combine slides in different ways, they still have the pieces of the story, and they can easily prepare themselves to tell it convincingly. You also might consider inviting salespeople to upload their compilations of slide decks with a description about what they used them for and how the presentation affected their audience. Providing the raw materials is terrific. Inviting salespeople to share the ways they put them to best use gives the rest of the team access to proven tools.

One of the reasons I used slides in the preceding examples is that it's easy to copy and paste slide material into a Word document or even select from a slide library and then create a .pdf file in addition to creating a relevant meeting presentation. The key to creating marketing content that your salespeople actually will use is collaboration.

To get started, take a sampling of your recent sales, and learn which collateral those salespeople used to close the sale. Ask them what they would've liked to have but didn't that might have enabled them to shorten the sales cycle. Yes, the answers will vary widely based on the individual salesperson's style, industry, and product focus. This is why it's easiest to use small content slices. Such slices are more flexible and can be combined in a number of ways. In addition, your buyers' attention spans are shorter and more discriminating, and no two sales will be exactly the same. Maintaining consistency by matching sales messaging with buyer expectations set at the beginning of the relationship keeps buyers moving forward.

## PART VI

# MEANINGFUL METRICS

Quantitative measures can prove marketing's business impact.

## Chapter 18

# Quantifying Marketing Results

Quantifying eMarketing strategy value is a good reason to invest in marketing automation technology that not only helps to improve interaction relevance with prospects but also provides valuable metrics. Among other things, theses metrics can prove that the marketing budget is based on wise investments that produce returns to both the top line and the bottom.

Digital marketing and technologies are enabling marketers to finally prove their contribution to their company's attainment of strategic objectives. Marketers now can prove impact to sales goals as well as measure their engagement progress to continually improve contributions to sales achievements.

Salespeople are focused on meeting quotas based on specific short-window time frames. Their value is simpler to measure. Marketing goals must include both short-window and longer-term results that map to sales goals. Thankfully, it's no longer necessary for one to be sacrificed for the achievement of the other. One of the biggest challenges for marketers has been demonstrating the impact of marketing programs on sales efficiency and, ultimately, revenues.

Technology offers the tools to track marketing's impact on the entire buying process—from sales transition through revenue. Marketers can create and implement metrics to evidence their impact on the velocity of closed deals. With this proof, marketing becomes a valued service to the business based on contribution, not speculation.

Measurable eMarketing strategies provide you and your company with a better read on the market and the buying process. To continuously improve engagement that progresses buying behavior, marketers also must measure progressive goals that show they're on the right track. By monitoring short- and longer-term prospect movement, marketing has its fingers on the pulse and sentiment of your buyers. As marketers develop historical benchmarks, they can see the shifts in buying behavior and respond in real time, eliminating surprises. Imagine being able to know that the tipping point for demand is increasing. Your company can increase manufacturing in time to meet a spike in demand. Or what if you have the visibility to see that prospects who appeared interested are pulling back? You have the chance to learn why their priorities have shifted and take proactive steps to address those changes—ahead of the competition.

Producing meaningful metrics not only helps marketers improve their ability to make progressive connections with prospects, but it also gives marketing the capacity to impact customer acquisition rates and lifecycle outcomes. Marketing needs to measure the impact of eMarketing strategies from beginning to end. By measuring progressively, marketers gain the intelligence to make improvements to engagement, ensuring their eMarketing strategy contributes effectively to sales results at the end of the buying process.

## ENGAGEMENT METRICS

The willingness of prospects to consistently interact with your content and communications must be measured. Increasing their level of interest is a determinant of how well you'll progress prospects to sales readiness. By monitoring and measuring your prospects' actions in response to your eMarketing, you can continuously improve the volume of qualified prospects you hand over to sales.

### *Scoring for Engagement*

Scoring has a number of applications. The best known is digital prospect activity captured iteratively to create a prospect profile that indicates sales readiness. Scoring for engagement during nurturing is different from scoring for impact on sales. Nurturing scores note prospect engagement levels, dialogue, and the pull from origination sources that produce the best demand generation for opt-in programs. First, however, let's take a look at content calibration. Since content is a primary component of the execution of your eMarketing strategies, it needs to be evolved continuously based on how well it meets prospects' needs. By monitoring how your content is accessed and used by prospects, you've got the insights you need to build productive relationships.

### *Content Calibration*

Just because you've created marketing content designed to answer the needs of your prospects, customers, and salespeople doesn't mean that it's doing what it should. Every piece of content you create is designed with a goal in mind. Unless you measure against that goal, you won't know if your content "scored" or missed by a mile. Assessing how well your content performs against the goals it's designed to achieve, the role it plays in extending prospect interest, and determining how often content is passed along to others are indications of engagement.

**Goal Achievement**   Your content will be designed to achieve any of a number of goals, including getting opt-in for a download, clicks on a hyperlink, registration for a Webinar, viewing of a demo, subscription to an e-mail series, or the submission of an inquiry form. Great content often can accomplish more than one goal. For example, if a number of prospects are reading the article, clicking on a specific embedded hyperlink, opting-in for a newsletter subscription, or registering for a Webinar on a related subject, take a careful look at that content to learn how you can transform other content to produce such great results.

---

**TIPS FOR MONITORING GOAL ACHIEVEMENT**

- Click-stream metrics showing what prompts prospects to access content provide insight to triggers that increase attention.
- Monitor the storyline content you've created for each target segment. If pieces of a storyline are being skipped by most prospects, revise them, and measure changes in response. Or replace the content with an extension to another piece that's generating more interest.
- Measure each type of call to action you're using to learn which cues encourage the highest response levels. For example, if Webinar registrations motivate more responses than other offers, create more of them. Every time a prospect responds, he is telling you what interests him.
- Topics that get the most attention are clues for further content development that helps to build engagement.
- The number of opt-ins to newsletters, content series, and event registrations increases your sphere of influence. But opting-in is only the first step. You need to see a corresponding growth in response levels to your eMarketing.

*( Continued )*

> - Monitor opt-outs and participation levels. If people register for but don't attend your Webinars, are they accessing the archived version at a later date? Are they subscribing to your newsletter but not attracted back to your Web site to read the content when they receive the monthly issue?

**Embedded Hyperlink Activity**   Let's say that you've created a collection of content for one stage of the buying process, linking the pieces with hyperlinks within the text of each piece. You've also provided sidebar navigation to the other pieces in the collection. Are prospects following the storyline the way you laid it out, or are you seeing navigational paths that are different? If the hyperlinks are in the top third of the content, are prospects spending enough time to read that page first and then click, or are they bouncing from page to page without showing much engagement? The better you get at telling valuable stories, the more active your prospects will become in following them through to the end. This is progressive engagement.

Once you've gotten people to engage with your content, you want them to interact with more of it. Placing links strategically to pull readers through related content helps you to build engagement and progress them farther. When you create groups of content, linked together, measuring the number of readers who access all of it is an indication of interest levels and higher engagement.

---

### TIPS FOR INCREASING LINK RESPONSE

- Change the words in your hyperlinks to make them more active.
- Move the hyperlink to a different place in the content that's a more natural extension for the reader.
- Alter the descriptions or titles used in the sidebar links to catch readers there if the hyperlinks don't.
- Assess the keywords Web-site visitors are using to find your content, and revise your content to use those keywords as your hyperlink text.

---

**Pass-Along Value**   The most common measurement of pass-along is use of the "Forward to a friend" functionality at corporate Web sites. However, pass-along value has evolved. It's measurable by monitoring inbound links from other sites such as StumbleUpon,

Digg, and Delicious; other blogs; industry aggregate sites; and Twitter. Google Alerts are a good way to track pass-along value, as well as the metrics for referring sites tracked in your Web analytics programs. Consider using a link-shortening service such as budURL, which allows you to track the click stream produced by the links you post to external Web sites or social platforms.

Referrals are a primary source of prospects most likely to become customers. If someone they trust refers them to your content to help them solve a problem, prospects will engage more actively with your company. If they see your content at the online sites they frequent, your credibility will increase, and they'll remember you when they need a vendor with your expertise. The syndication of articles, e-books, and white papers on industry Web sites helps to increase awareness for your company. Submit education and expertise content to industry Web sites your prospects frequent. People who find your content valuable will link to it in their blog posts, share a link to the article on Twitter, or send that link to a colleague whom they know will be interested.

Pass-along value is a strong reason to consider blogging as a thought leader in your market space. Blog posts serve several purposes for gaining pass-along exposure to your content. They are indexed quickly in search engines, linked to by other bloggers writing about the same topics, and invite comments from readers.

---

### TIPS FOR INCREASING PASS-ALONG

- Focus your content on business issues relevant to your prospects.
- Take a controversial stand–people love to stir the pot.
- Show prospects how to take action–how-to guides have traction.
- Create executive summaries for e-books, reports, and white papers that help prospects share the value points with others easily.
- Monitor content placement to focus your online content distribution to places that produce the highest engagement levels.

---

Calibrating your content helps to make sure that it's doing its job by connecting with prospects, influencers, and customers. Content audits that measure effectiveness should be done regularly to monitor engagement levels. The only way to know is to assess and refine your content on a proactive basis.

## ORIGINATION SOURCES FOR OPT-IN PROGRAMS

Opt-in programs are the lifeblood of demand generation. It's no longer effective to rent or purchase lists of prospects who haven't given you direct permission to contact them. Instead, your company needs to become a preferred choice for content that addresses priorities on your prospects' radar. The ubiquity of the Internet enables marketers to attract new and larger audiences to interact with your company.

The best opt-in programs are associated with a value delivered to your prospects. High-value offers promoting your expertise at solving prospect problems include Webinars, private appointments at trade shows, e-newsletter subscriptions, white papers, and special-report download offers. Really Simple Syndication (RSS) feeds and widgets are also compelling. Offers for opt-in can be promoted via your blog, corporate Web site, targeted microsites, special content offers included with articles posted on industry e-zine sites, and Pay Per Click (PPC) ads on search engines.

Origination sources vary in their ability to generate demand. Monitoring them to determine the best producing sources is one way to tune and improve effectiveness. The responses generated by origination sources can help you to define valid market segments and prove that you're in the right place to engage them. Even better is when you can tie customer acquisition back to origination sources. It doesn't matter if you generate 100 or thousands of opt ins from an origination source if none of those prospects ever buy from you.

---

### TIPS FOR OPT-IN PROGRAMS

- Measure the traffic generated by external origination sources compared with the number of resulting prospect opt-ins.
- Monitor the growth in engagement scores for those prospects. Do they progress faster or more slowly than other prospects?

*(Continued)*

- Pinpoint which program drives the highest number of opt-ins, and create exposure on similar Web properties.
- Tie customer acquisition back to opt-in programs to prove the value of the origination source.
- Terminate programs on origination sources that deliver high traffic but a low number of quality opt-ins.

### Recognize Shifting Priorities and Stop Leakage

Buyers are focused on answering their highest-priority issues. Priorities have a lot of flex. What's important this month may be less important next month. Marketing must monitor for triggering events that shift priorities. It's possible that a triggering event can affect all your prospects—such as the case of an economic downturn—but it's more likely that triggering events for one segment may not affect the others to the same extent. For example, a compliance regulation with a fast-approaching deadline for one industry may not come into play for another.

If a triggering event causes priorities to shift, then content must shift as well to avoid leakage. Measuring leakage from your nurturing programs isn't enough on its own. Determining what causes the leaks provides insights that you can use to stop them.

## MEASURES HIGHLIGHTING SHIFTING PRIORITIES
## THAT CAUSE LEAKAGE

- Frequency of activity declines
- Lengthening time between interactions
- Opt-outs
- Reduced participation in once-popular programs

With the right measures, you can take proactive steps to reverse the damage before there is any significant impact. For example:

- If you see frequency of activity decline, learn which prospect profiles it's affecting. Then take a look at that market segment and find out what's changed for those prospects. Salespeople who sell into that segment also can be helpful in providing information from the street to help you diagnose the issue. Reevaluate your approach, and tune it to meet the changes you discover.

- Lengthening time between interactions and opt-outs both indicate diminished interest. Move these prospects to a reactivation program in case their topical interest has changed. Make sure that you degrade their scores based on length of inactivity. For example, if they remain dormant for three months, you can reduce their score by 25 points. If they continue their dormant state for five months, you can choose to move them to a reactivation campaign to jumpstart them or move them to a keep-in-touch program and let them reactivate when they're ready. Measuring your prospects based on activity versus dormancy is a good indication of the effectiveness of your marketing programs.
- Measuring the reduction of participation in once-popular programs enables marketers to identify topics that have lost their luster. For example, if you held a Webinar that achieved outstanding participation levels and decide to run it again but get a much lower interest level, something else is at the top of your prospects' radar. Doing the same thing you've always done and expecting the same— or improved—results isn't a given in this fast-changing business environment.

Marketers who can demonstrate an ability to reduce leakage from the funnel by adjusting their eMarketing strategies to reignite engagement with prospects can prove to their companies that they know their customers. Learning what's shifted and tying that with sales feedback helps marketers to adjust personas and buying synopses to ensure that eMarketing programs stay on track. Demonstrating marketing's responsiveness creates value by producing a steady engagement level with quality prospects.

## MARKETING'S IMPACT ON SALES

Scoring for impact is based on evaluating shifts in momentum through the buying process. It involves assessing the volume of qualified sales-ready opportunities, as well as the impact on deal progression and reduced time to revenue. These metrics need to measure marketing's contribution and not be based on sales metrics geared for short time frames. Trying to measure marketing results by sales metrics defeats their longer-term purpose and creates an ongoing crazy cycle that dictates moving things along faster—according to the company's schedule, not the buyer's. Marketing that stretches farther into the sales process increases measurable contributions, demonstrating impact on sales.

### *Increasing Prospect Momentum*

An eMarketing strategy serves to increase momentum for your prospects in their buying process, accelerating the time to sales-ready transitions. Content designed for story flow can effectively shorten the time prospects spend in nurturing by delivering the right information at the right time.

Complex sales cycles are shown to be lengthening. When marketing grows prospect engagement with high-value information, the number of outreach touches necessary prior to conversion can be reduced. Prospects will proactively seek out your content and initiate interactions with your company. Interactive dialogues that enable marketers to answer the additional needs of prospects during buying stages will help prospects to stay engaged and keep them moving forward. When marketers monitor and tune their ability to create and sustain valued engagement, prospects are highly qualified when the transition to sales occurs. And sales will return less of them to marketing.

---

**MEASURE MARKETING'S IMPACT ON MOMENTUM**

- Length of time spent in nurturing
- Number of outreach touches before sales-ready qualification
- Number of inbound conversations with prospects per time period
- Number of interactive dialogues with prospects who transition to sales
- Number of prospects returned to nurturing by sales

---

The best eMarketing programs will encourage interactions with prospects to increase the momentum of their decisions to buy. The following prospect behaviors demonstrate increasing momentum:

- Prospects' buying behavior may be accelerating if they're returning to your Web site or microsite to revisit content they've viewed previously, accessing additional resources, or proactively accessing content focused on one storyline. Create alerts for marked increases in content access or the frequency of visits to initiate a personalized interaction and learn what else prospects need. Note which content is being accessed proactively, and learn how to adjust other content to create that attraction quality.
- Prospects who request more information are increasing their momentum. Learn what prompted the inquiry, and use that knowledge to adjust other nurturing tracks and calls to action to increase that behavior.
- An increase in participatory behavior—such as attending multiple Webinars in a compressed time frame, viewing demos, or using value calculators—should alert marketing to nudge prospects to the next step.

With attention paid to prospect behavior, marketing can move to increase momentum through the marketing funnel. Focusing on what prospects need ensures that the momentum is generated proactively by the prospect and corresponds to a higher quality of sales readiness.

### Volume of Sales-Ready Opportunities

There are several things to consider when measuring volume. If, in the past, marketing provided 300 prospects per month to the sales team, and those prospects yielded five deals, it doesn't necessarily follow that to get 15 deals, marketing would need to supply sales with 900 prospects. Instead, look at how many of the 300 prospects salespeople actually followed up with, what activities they pursued, and which messaging they used. Learn why they didn't follow up with the others. And make sure that any prospects not ready to buy are returned to the nurturing process. Reductions in the number of returned prospects should mean that salespeople are engaging with more of them and, ultimately, closing more deals.

Volume doesn't necessarily equal an increased number of complex sales. Qualified buyers do. The more sales ready prospects are, the better are the outcomes from sales activities. Monitor how many leads a salesperson engages with during a specific period and how many of them become customers. Learning how salespeople both work with and address opportunities can help marketing to create a "sales activity" nurturing process to ensure that no prospect gets left behind. Matching volume with sales capacity is critical for extending the relationships marketing has begun into satisfied, long-term customers.

---

### MEASURES TO TUNE VOLUME

- Number of sales-ready prospects each salesperson is actively working
- Deal stage for the prospects with whom a salesperson is working
- Time to first contact by salesperson after a handoff
- Number of prospects in the sales pipeline who haven't been touched in 30 days
- Reasons for the return of prospects to nurturing programs

---

Volume of pipeline is one key to sales. Marketing and sales must work together to create the right amount of volume to optimize close ratios by capitalizing on the momentum of prospects at the time of handoff. By measuring sales communications and ensuring handoffs are pursued quickly, marketing can step in and help to ensure sales-ready prospects continue making progress. Learning why prospects are returned to nurturing can help marketing increase quality levels so that salespeople are working deals that progress to purchase.

### *Deal Progression*

Metrics must focus on the entire sales process—from initial communication through close—or return to nurturing. It's especially important to note step-backs that stall a buyer from moving forward and ensure that salespeople are armed with the content they need to answer doubts, remove obstacles, and get that deal back in progress.

To show an impact on shortening buying cycles, you need to benchmark the average number of days buyers spend with your sales team from the time of transition, the number and types of interactions the salesperson has with buyers, their use of marketing-developed content, and where the stalls or accelerators happen. If the time a buyer spends with sales is benchmarked at 60 days, define the process and content improvements to accelerate closure—to 45 days, for example.

Just as marketing provides a prospect activity profile to sales at the handoff, so should sales provide a history of activity taken with a prospect during the sales process. Compare sales-activity histories of deals that close with deals that don't. Note the timing and communications during the escalation of activity, as well as the slowdowns. Learn the reasons for both, and note how sales reps responded. Compile best practices from closed deals, and use those insights to speed deal progression overall.

Audit the sales tools you're providing to salespeople, and make adjustments to improve underperforming content. Determine if any nurturing steps can be added prior to handoff to reduce the incidence of stalls. If the reason for the stalls is consistent, revisit your personas and buyer synopses to make adjustments. Apply any necessary adjustments to the agreed on definition of a sales-ready prospect.

Shortening time to revenue is a key area for marketing impact, and it's an improvement your sales team, executive team, and chief financial officer will find extremely valuable.

### Downstream Revenue Contribution

The bottom-line impact measures are truly the most important to marketing and to the overall company. These include the number and value of sales that can be traced back to a prospect nurtured by marketing and passed on to sales when qualified. You also can measure additional details such as faster time to sale, greater margins from sales, and overall sales efficiency. When salespeople are able to spend more time in face-to-face conversations with buyers because their administrative prep time is reduced dramatically, marketing is also reducing bottom-line costs.

Showing a consistent reduction in the number of days prospects spend in the marketing-to-sales process is an indication of marketing impact. Measure the total time spent, the time in nurturing, and the time spent with sales activities to gain visibility on where the improvements are occurring during the buyers' journey to get the full picture.

---

**MEASURES OF CONTRIBUTION TO DOWNSTREAM REVENUES**

- Number of marketing-produced prospects who purchased
- Number of sales-produced prospects who purchased
- Dollar amount of deals
- Margin on the deal
- Length of time in marketing-to-sales process
- Customer lifetime value

---

Compare the deals closed with marketing-produced prospects and those initiated by sales. It's likely that, on average, the dollar amounts and margins are both higher on marketing-produced prospects. This is so because of the value delivered by nurturing programs. The higher the value and expert advisory capability ascribed to your company, the less prospects will argue for discounts. When the payoffs for them are high, the best investment in expertise to get those results is perceived as worthwhile. A prospect who becomes a customer with this kind of value interpretation is likely to stay loyal longer and spend more over time with your company.

## Chapter 19

# Opportunity Quality and Sales Results

e Marketing strategies change the way salespeople interact with prospects when they are designed to engage, educate, and help solve problems. When your salespeople deliver on the expectations marketing has put into play, more deals are closed. And this is a meaningful metric.

Consistent, relevant e-interactions will increase your buyers' expectations about the relationship they'll develop with your company. Products have become the side benefit from choosing a vendor. What's taking precedence are the ideas, insights, and knowledge that, when applied to your products, deliver long-term and high-impact business results.

When knowledge about buyers is up-to-date, salespeople will sell more easily. Buyers do notice. They have no interest in or patience for spending their valuable time educating salespeople. They're looking for ideas and insights that apply specifically to their business situations. If salespeople don't know buyers, their conversations often miss the mark.

The challenge is in keeping up with a number of changing dynamics, including your marketplace, buyers' priorities, industry trends, and even how your customers' customers are evolving. Just when you think you know your market, it will shift. This is the reality of doing business today. New technologies, closer collaboration with peers, the blurring of global boundaries—all these, and more, will cause your prospects and customers to reevaluate how they choose to solve their problems or how they view the possibilities for achieving competitive advantage.

Changes happen quickly and often with quiet subtlety. Those who aren't looking and listening will miss golden opportunities for differentiation, innovation, and unprecedented growth. Marketers who stay firmly attuned to present needs, with an eye to the future, have the opportunity to help salespeople engage in compelling conversations. And that is what keeps your sales force selling.

## OPPORTUNITY QUALITY

As marketing tunes and improves the way prospects are evaluated and scored, the quality of the opportunities that marketing transitions to sales improves. Although quality is thought of as a subjective definition, when both sales and marketing are aligned in their definition of what a qualified buyer looks like, consistency is achieved.

---

### MEASURES OF OPPORTUNITY QUALITY

- Number of marketing-produced opportunities accepted by the sales team
- Number of contacts needed to complete a first sales conversation/meeting
- Number of monthly meetings scheduled with marketing-produced opportunities
- Number of active stakeholders within an opportunity company participating in dialogue

---

Salespeople will find that well-qualified opportunities know their company and more readily engage in conversation with them. Because fewer contact attempts are required to schedule a meeting, the number of meetings and conversations salespeople can achieve increases with opportunity quality. Because marketers have enlarged their scope of reach across stakeholders, salespeople also should have a higher ability to connect with multiple people from that company to move the buying process forward.

Specific to sales activities, the number of dialogues and meetings salespeople are able to schedule and hold with sales-ready prospects marketing has given them should be measured. "Face time" is important. When marketing-produced opportunities are allowing salespeople to get their foot in the door faster than the time it takes to accomplish the same thing from sales-generated prospects, marketing efforts are producing higher-value and greater-efficiency outcomes for the sales process. If it used to take three attempts to get a conversation and now it takes one, this shift can produce shorter time to revenue.

## SALES RESULTS

When marketing achieves quantifiable results, the nature of sales processes changes. The sales side of the buying process improves based on the impact marketing makes on the top of the funnel.

### Time to Revenue

Shortening sales cycles is a critical imperative for both sales and marketing. The current trend is for sales cycles to expand rather than contract. However, there's a growing amount of evidence that shows nurtured prospects buy more often and faster and spend more than those with minimal interactions with your company.

---

#### MEASURES TO ASSESS TIME TO REVENUE

- Days a prospect spends in nurturing
- Days a prospect spends with salespeople
- Buying stages when marketing acquires prospects
- Speed of progression through buying stages
- Number of step-backs unrecoverable by salespeople that return buyers to nurturing

---

By assessing at which buying stage your prospects opt-in, you can begin benchmarking how long they spend in nurturing and which activities indicate progressive movement to the next buying stage. Marketing can define particular triggers that indicate momentum and determine what's moving your buyers forward. Monitoring step-backs is another metric that helps you to improve time-to-revenue outcomes. If you see a trend developing that will cause prospects to be returned to nurturing by your sales team, marketers can address the issue head-on. By working with salespeople, marketing can develop content and communications to help prospects return their focus to solving their problem with your company's help.

Marketing must assume a greater responsibility for moving prospects farther through the pipeline. Highly qualified prospects spend less time with salespeople before they buy. The result is that your sales team becomes focused on selling to prospects who are actively buying in shorter time frames.

### Sales Wins

> ## MEASURES OF MARKETING'S IMPACT ON SALES
>
> - Percentage of wins from marketing-produced opportunities
> - Percentage of nondecision outcomes from marketing-produced opportunities
> - Number of cross-sell and up-sell sales to existing customers
> - Number of turnaround sales orchestrated by marketing programs
> - Deal dollar amounts realized from marketing-produced opportunities in comparison with previous deal sizes
> - Margins realized from marketing-produced opportunity wins
> - Number of entry-level versus full-solution sales to marketing-produced opportunities

This is, of course, the big-deal metric. Sales generated from marketing-produced leads should increase, nondecisions should decrease, and existing customer follow-on sales should be on the rise. Turnarounds occur when marketing takes back a prospect not ready to buy, reengages him, and requalifies the prospect for sales activities. Such wins should be noted separately to show the impact eMarketing programs have on prospects who step back. Measures based on the reason for the step-backs also can help to improve this restart process.

Prospects who consider your company a trusted advisor are less influenced by price. Your prospects' perception of the value and expertise your company provides trumps concern over price. When marketing can show that the sales-ready prospects they produce not only buy more but also spend more, this is a proof point that will carry a lot of weight. Being able to show impact to top-line revenues plus increasing customer profitability garners marketers' respect and bigger budgets. And it doesn't hurt one bit that salespeople are seeing bigger commissions.

### Sales Overhead Time

A number of surveys and research reports have benchmarked the time salespeople spend in non-revenue-producing activities. Active selling time ranges from 20 to 40 percent. This means that most of their time is not spent selling. Marketing can reduce sales overhead dramatically with the right eMarketing strategy and process.

Behavior often speaks louder than words. Using a combination of both sales feedback and measurement helps marketing to prove their impact on reducing overhead time.

---

### MEASURES OF SALES EFFICIENCY

- Number of overall meetings/conversations salespeople had with buyers
- Number of follow-on meetings salespeople had with buyers
- Number of prospects generated by salespeople
- Time spent cold calling
- Time spent researching new business opportunities
- Ramp time for new salespeople or for existing salespeople with new products
- Salesperson feedback forms
- Overall sales portal use
- Use of marketing-generated messaging in sales communications

---

An increase in the number of meetings salespeople have with buyers is a key indication of less time spent on nonselling activities. By reducing overhead time, sales reps also should be able to engage in quality conversations with a higher volume of qualified prospects, expanding their opportunity to win business.

Your salespeople also should show a decline in the time spent on demand generation and cold calling owing to the volume of qualified prospects marketing is providing. Proof this can happen is evident in both the Marketo and HubSpot stories showcased in earlier chapters.

Salesperson feedback forms can be used to prove that your salespeople are finding value from marketing-produced sales content and nurturing activities. Tying the forms to won deals, as well as losses, can highlight both the great content and the content that needs improvement. If marketing has improved the quality of sales content and the ways in which salespeople can find and use it, this metric should show increased sales portal usage that equates to a reduction of time spent on administrative tasks.

However, it's not just eliminating time spent searching for and recreating content that's important. The CMO Council found that fewer than 25 percent of chief marketing officers and sales vice presidents were satisfied with their salespeople's ability to articulate value.[1] By employing marketing-generated messaging, sales reps not only have better conversations, but they also can get up to speed more quickly on new product messaging and value. Salespeople recreate content based on their viewpoints. When the messaging they use is consistent with the story prospects have already been told, no confusion is introduced that can lengthen the buying process. The impact of telling a consistent story from the beginning to the end of the buying process pays off with higher buyer confidence that leads to more sales wins.

## Chapter 20

# Feedback and Dialogue

C ontinuously producing highly relevant and valuable content can be seen as a top challenge by marketers. Sixty-one percent of B2B marketers surveyed rate developing Web 2.0 content as a top or important priority. However, 81 percent find the development of that content very or somewhat challenging.[1] Producing one slate of content may seem tough enough, but to have to augment that storyline repeatedly with new stories that feed your company's overarching theme can seem an unwieldy proposition. However, it doesn't have to be. Once you've set the foundational principles for your eMarketing strategies, you've got the potential to put all the tools in place to make relevant and fresh content development a perpetual process.

In the digital age, marketing content is designed around conversational interactions. The fuel for your content is right in front of you with your customers and the dialogues you hold with prospects. By incorporating customer and prospect feedback and dialogues into your content, you'll ensure that each article, blog post, and Webinar is relevant and valuable.

Think about it:

- You're customer-focused. Every eMarketing initiative is designed from the customer's perspective.
- You've listened to the market and applied what you've heard.
- You've mined feedback from interactions for new ideas. You're prepared to create stories about how your company can bring those ideas to life.
- You've personalized your content and approaches, and prospects have responded. In fact, they think you're speaking directly to them.

The sources for ongoing story generation are infinite, many of them right at your fingertips. Internal resources include your customers, salespeople, support and service staff, and product-development teams. External resources include influential and customer bloggers on related topics, prospects, industry analysts, and even your competitors. The keys are to make sure you're consistent, that each new story has a place within your overall story theme, and that you continue to evolve that theme with each story.

Showing that marketing is increasing the interactive dialogue held with prospects and customers is a measure of engagement. Proof that your content is provoking responses in the form of questions, comments, and interactions means the relationships you're building have higher potential to become sales ready. We've already shown how to use feedback and dialogue to measure marketing from a quantitative perspective. It's equally important to use feedback and dialogue as a source of perpetual ideas for ongoing content development.

## IN TUNE AND IN TOUCH

Now that you've developed an eMarketing foundation with a story slate, don't think that you're finished. Embracing storytelling means you're continuously evolving stories. To sit still means risking irrelevance. And that's something you can't afford— not when your prospects are expecting more stories from you.

Marketers now have the means and the tools to stay in tune and in touch. Constant and continuous monitoring of feedback from a variety of sources will keep you up-to-date. You'll be able to see the impact of current storylines and gather the fuel to create new ones.

### Feedback for Content Development

**Salespeople**   Your sales team spends more time speaking with your potential customers than anyone else. When eliciting their feedback about street-level interactions with buyers, make sure that you look for specific insights to either create new stories or tune existing ones. Look for issues or concerns your content may not be addressing. Consider allowing salespeople to comment on and rate sales collateral and content on your sales portal to learn more. Pay attention to the conversational nuances you hear. They can help you to create content that produces higher engagement.

**Prospects**   You gain valuable insights every time you get a response to your eMarketing. Comments made on your corporate blog, customers' blogs, or industry blogs are also fodder for new ideas. When your company attends trade shows or speaks at conferences, be sure to ask questions about what's top-of-mind today. What you learn can enable the creation of a number of new stories to address evolving prospect needs.

Webinars are a great way to stay in tune. Every question asked by a participant has the potential of a related story idea or follow-on Webinar. Questions can be indications of where gaps exist in the information your prospects need. When a prospect asks a question, the question and how it was answered also should be added to that prospect's profile as background information. You also may learn more about the prospect's buying stage. When scoring your prospects, assign points for Webinar registration, attendance, and questions asked.

**Customers**   Many companies survey customers about satisfaction. But customer surveys can do more than gather great references and quotes.

Focus on collecting customer information that improves your company, not just pats you on the back. Don't just interview longer-term customers for success stories. Interview those who aren't seeing the success they wanted, and find out why not. Customers who still need help provide ideas for stories about issues your prospects may face that they haven't connected with the original problem. Some issues don't surface until after the implementation. Think longer term.

These experiences can become holistic stories developed to help your existing customers to better use your products and solutions. They also can provide fodder for thought-leadership articles that help your potential customers better evaluate and mitigate risk in deciding how to answer their challenges.

**Customer Support and Service Staff**   Your call center, help desk, and support staff usually are the ones in closest contact with your customers after the sale and implementation. Use their insights to ensure your marketing content is focused on relevant issues. Not only can you glean ideas for ongoing story development, but you also can prepare your service staff with questions that help your company continue to "know" your customers better than before. Add these insights to your personas and segmentation strategies to make sure that you're in tune with what's happening outside the walls of your company.

## STORY IDEAS FROM THIRD PARTIES

Many B2B companies with complex sales that are faced with increasing their marketing content development opt to use third-party expertise content and provide it as a service to their prospects and customers. The problem with an approach that features outside experts is that if it's your only approach, you're becoming known as a provider of other people's thoughts, not as a thought leader in your own right.

Developing customer-focused content for a prospect-controlled buying process is a differentiating expertise. To develop relationships that position your company as an expert, you need to take the plunge. Not all at once, mind you, but authoring your own content has huge payoffs in engagement, credibility, and interactive dialogue. If you're only providing other people's content, your prospects won't want to talk with you; they'll want to talk to those people. And that defeats the point.

Third parties still offer some great opportunities for story generation. For example, measuring the impact of your content in comparison with third-party expertise content helps you to gauge how compelling your company is versus a true expert's insights. We've all done this. Who hasn't gotten an e-mail with the latest report by a research firm at the end of a link and filled out the form because the report was worth the effort? Then, when the company starts pelting you with e-mails, you either unsubscribe or assign them to the junk mail folder for quick deletion.

Consider, instead, that creating the content your prospects want is more personal. The relationship is being built between you and them. The opportunity to develop interactive dialogue is higher if there's a reason for prospects to reach out to you for more.

### Third-Party Resources

**Influential Bloggers**   The beauty of influential bloggers in your prospect communities is that they're usually talking about top-of-mind issues for their readers. They also tend to get a lot of comments. Their topics will give you ideas about issues of concern on the radar for your prospects. The comments made on their posts help you gain insight into the perspectives of the readers. Reading the comments will help you develop a tone your audience can relate to and help you to employ familiar phrases they use themselves. By clicking through on the links to commenters' names, you also can learn more about them or the company that employs them.

**Industry Analysts**   Every industry has analysts who are respected and followed for their insights. Sign up for e-mail notification about reports and press releases from several of the experts your prospects respect. Take note of the topics they're covering and the summary descriptions of new reports. Many analyst companies also have blogs. Monitoring them can provide a wealth of ideas. Chances are that whatever they're talking about are subjects which are top-of-mind for your prospects.

**Competitors**   Your competitors are also a great resource for content-development ideas. Press releases, new white papers, and customer stories can be sources of topics your company can put its spin on by applying your expertise to the subject differently. The key to doing this well is to make sure that you're not following the competition but leading readers to a fresh take that differentiates your company from others.

**Industry Publications/Web Sites**   Industry publications are a great resource for defining segment issues as well as learning more about general trend issues. With most of them online and updated often, these resources provide a steady flow of information and insights for story generation. Many of them also enable readers to submit comments in response to articles or rate them, providing additional insights. They're also media vehicles that may syndicate your company's thought-leadership articles and white papers.

## APPLIED LISTENING

There's a difference between listening and hearing. *Listening* means that you may be cognizant of what's being said. *Hearing* means that you understand what's being said from the perspective of the speaker. *Applied listening* is when you've listened, heard, and are now acting on that feedback to encourage ongoing dialogue.

Every input is worthy of evaluation, analysis, and appropriate response. Remember, eMarketing is about generating conversations. This means increasing the level of interactions between your company and your prospects. Responses need to address what you heard, not engineer a reply to suit what you want to say. Instead, consider measuring how well your responses increase the momentum of prospects through their buying process.

The goal with applied listening is to generate ongoing dialogue, not push the company's agenda. Your prospects care about, and will be more responsive to, interactions that provide valuable information and ideas that directly answer their needs, questions, and concerns. If your responses are not enticing prospects to move forward in their consideration of your company as their next vendor, this metric will tell you.

Figure 20.1 shows an example of a dialogue in action. The point of an interactive dialogue during marketing is to continue to exchange valuable information, not deliver a sales pitch. It's also about getting prospects to take next steps. In this example, the prospect proactively leaves a comment on your corporate blog. You now have the prospect's name and e-mail address. You respond to the comment and add a question that hopefully will entice the prospect to comment back. You also send the prospect an e-mail with a link to content on a topic related to the blog post. When the prospect downloads or accesses the content, you respond by sending her an invitation to a Webinar on that topic. Each action taken by the prospect generates an appropriate reaction on your part, guiding your relationship closer to sales readiness.

The idea is to keep the interactions going by increasing the value of the content and hopefully enticing the prospect to make forward progress by being helpful. Ask open-ended questions along with your communications to help you learn more about the prospect. And

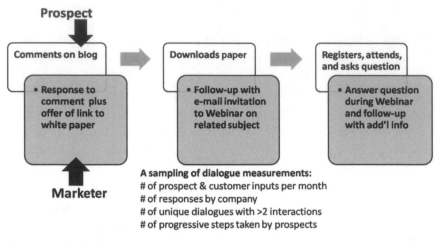

**Figure 20.1** Dialogue in action.

please don't pitch the sale. The prospect will let you know if she is ready to buy.

Dialogue metrics that show how well your eMarketing strategies attract prospects to interact with you are increasingly important for determining engagement levels. In a complex sale, where time to decision can be longer term, marketing needs metrics that show not only hard value achievement but also soft value momentum. Although some of these metrics are in their early stages, as you work with them, you'll begin to evolve how you determine levels of engagement and trust in your relationships and also improve your ability to detect the stage your prospect occupies in the buying process.

## IMPROVED PERSONALIZATION

Everything you learn about your prospects can be used to improve the way you personalize your eMarketing strategies to evolve your engagement metrics. Feedback comes from many different sources and is relevant, perhaps even more so, when it's not just about your company. Marketers need to think of feedback as response to topics in addition to direct responses to their efforts. You probably can learn more about your prospects through topic feedback than you can when they speak to you directly. Mostly this is due to an innate nature to maintain distance by skimming the surface of what we mean with what we choose to say.

An example is people who mark a survey with a less than satisfactory indicator but are unwilling to enter text about why they chose that rating. We don't generally like confrontation and do our best to avoid it, even when there's no reason why we should. Online interactions have started to change this. Being able to add comments on blog posts and contribute reviews and ratings of everything from books to travel to Twitter has made us braver. Many people have discovered the need to voice their opinions. And this is a boon for marketers. Instead of expensive focus groups, we now can find online discussion threads about specific topics of interest and monitor responses in real time.

Monitoring online conversations for personalization insights requires getting below the surface of the words to the meaning behind them. Personalization involves nuance, not just phrase agreement. During complex-sale marketing, personalization has meant that your content is addressed to roles or matched to industry. But this is not enough. For B2B eMarketing to become personal, the content and interactions have to appeal to the individual as well as to the professional. For some reason, we seem to have forgotten that business solutions buyers are also people.

Measuring your efforts at personalization is tricky. One way to do so is by assessing your ability to build credibility. Attaining higher levels of credibility is evidenced by your prospect's willingness to part with increasing amounts of information as well as engage in dialogue with you. Ask for too much at the beginning, and you'll get nothing because you haven't established the value of participation. However, if you consistently provide relevant content that your prospects find useful, they'll become more willing to divulge specifics truthfully. The operative word in this last sentence is *truthfully*. If your stories are well written, prospects begin to feel that they know your company. It becomes a real entity to them, imbued with characteristics they relate to.

Figure 20.2 illustrates how the process and measurement may look. Measure the number of prospects willing to provide increasing amounts of information. For example, if you have a content storyline

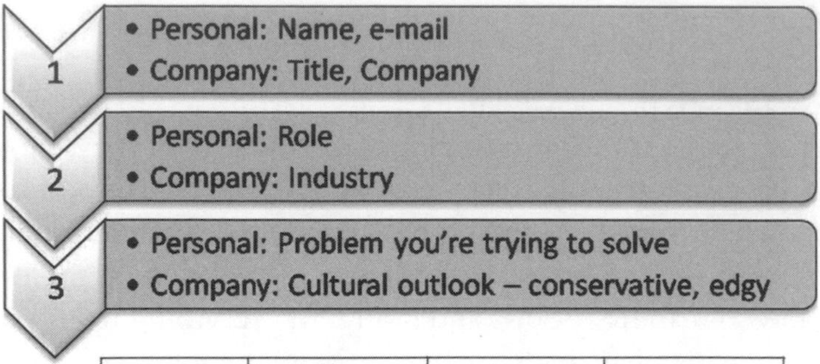

| Stage: | Month 1 | Month 2 | Month 3 |
|--------|---------|---------|---------|
| 1 | 150 | 187 | 218 |
| 2 | 42 | 60 | 81 |
| 3 | 17 | 28 | 45 |

**Figure 20.2** Progressive prospect trust.

that has three stages of information gathering, how many prospects progressed through all three? Improved personalization enables marketers of complex sales to gain a more accurate measurement of how trustworthy your company is perceived to be. The more information prospects are willing to part with in exchange for your content offers, the more interest they're expressing. And that's feedback that helps to create sales-ready prospects.

Feedback and dialogue are critical to today's marketer. Both internal and external resources can be used to help you create stories that drive engagement. Increasing your company's ability to sustain online dialogue with prospects is a measure of trust and credibility. In a world where relevance is king and engagement is driven by information that meets prospects' needs, embracing interactions as well as learning from them improves your ability to progress buyers toward purchase decisions. By showing a continuously increasing ability to engage prospects beyond just viewing content, marketing can add more proof that they're in touch with buyers and able to progress them farther into the pipeline.

## Chapter 21

# Social Contributions

Social media is the latest entry to the marketing mix—more so right now for individuals than brands. Soon, however, the new conversational mentality will require companies to empower employees to carry the company's expertise into the world and participate through social media. It's tough for a company to participate on its own. It needs people to carry the story. If the company tries to engage in conversations without humanizing itself, prospects will hesitate. Get started by listening to your customers; then branch out to your prospects. You'll gain traction and clarity with an iterative approach.

What is clear is that companies must join the conversation to create sustainable growth as the number of online environments and connection possibilities expands. The biggest difference today is that people are empowered to communicate online with those whom they might never have "met" otherwise. Ideas spread quickly. People are talking up a storm about whatever interests them. They're asking questions and getting feedback from a multitude of sources—both company-related and individual.

The important thing to realize is that social networking isn't an all-or-nothing proposition. You can stick your toe in. You can listen and begin participating with honesty and integrity, and ramp up your efforts as you become more comfortable. Credibility in the future will be focused on the difference people say you make—the value you provide that's worth mentioning to others.

For social media to provide you with the optimal impact, it should be integrated into your eMarketing strategies. This means you need to develop a way to tie it to marketing goals. Measuring the impact of social media on its own is not yet a defined science. That said, you'll begin to evolve some tangible data that show how your social media efforts are impacting your online marketing programs if you think about it strategically in relation to your marketing mix, apply goals, and measure outcomes.

Social activities have the potential to be influential, not actual sales channels for a complex sale. They can be instrumental in attracting new audiences to your company and opening new threads of conversation. The B2B complex sale is still reliant on salespeople to close, and rightly so because expertise is needed for appropriate implementation, and a lot of money is at stake.

The benefits of social media for companies with complex sales are not limited to but certainly include

- Sharing expertise through personal interactions
- Humanizing your company
- Increasing awareness of your company's story
- Netting great ideas
- Building personalized relationships
- Gaining insights into prospect attributes
- Learning about and improving customer experiences
- Attracting new audiences to self-identify and opt-in

Social contributions can add impact, increase credibility, and validate your eMarketing program's ability to build engagement. As long as your presence within social media platforms is about helping—not pitching—your company has the opportunity to transform how prospects find, engage with, and choose your product offerings.

## VIRTUAL ENGAGEMENT

When you share great ideas that spread online, you have the opportunity to attract more qualified prospects, especially if you provide access to relevant content and participate in the resulting dialogue. Social media provides a platform for helpful expression. However, if used incorrectly, dissent can be swift and brutal. As long as you're focused on providing relevance and value, without being pushy or disrespectful, you'll find a warm reception.

Virtual engagement depends on personalized interactions. When you know your company's story theme, you can carry that tone and style across to a company presence or even have it reflected in the passion of the employees and customers who interact with others about your company online. This is the time to be individual and unique—not to sound like everyone else.

To benefit from the viral behavior of others, your content must include ideas people want to talk about and share. It's got to be considered valuable from the audience's perspective. A number of companies do this really well. Two examples in this book are Hub-

Spot and Marketo. Both these companies work tirelessly to provide content that helps their customers and prospective customers to solve issues that are top-of-mind in relation to the reasons people need their products in the first place. But there's a distinction that sets them apart. Both companies do so regardless of whether or not you buy from them.

They openly solicit feedback and invite conversations within social networks, and both companies provide valuable, fresh, and highly relevant content on a consistent basis. Through their employees who interact with others online, the companies have developed individualized personalities. You wouldn't mistake either of them for another "similar" company. Both Mike Volpe and Jon Miller and their staffs work tirelessly to keep delivering innovative content their audiences want and respond to. And both companies are growing remarkably fast—even during a time of economic uncertainty.

## PARTICIPATION SPEAKS VOLUMES

*Participation* refers to the responses, interactions, and dialogue your natural-nurturing campaigns and content motivate. Marketers need to be conversationally prepared to interact with prospects in as close to real time as possible. These interactions need to be focused on being helpful and extending the value delivered by whatever content or outreach attracted the prospects to your company. Participation is like intelligence gathering. Every interaction you have with prospects can be a valid source of insight that helps you to tune your story to match their needs. And knowing sure beats guessing.

Participation is often difficult for B2B marketers who haven't embraced the fact that their customers and prospects are now in control of the conversation, along with their buying journey. It requires an outward-in focus. It's also important not to forget that participation is a two-way street. It's not just about your comment on a blog post or a Twitter response with a URL that directs someone to your content. Participation is about developing a style and openness that encourages others to initiate interactions with you and your company. Quit thinking about your prospects as the vice president of whatever, and start thinking about them as Mary, Joe, and Sam. Just because it's a B2B complex sale doesn't mean you're only dealing with their profession. People buy from people they like and trust.

### Peer-to-Peer Conversations

A *peer* is someone who is considered to be equal to another in relation to the context of the interaction. People put more trust in people "like" them than in any other source of information. They're more inclined to respond to someone they consider to be a peer than they would to someone considered more impersonally—such as a marketer or salesperson. This is why context, tone, and style are so important to content and communication development—even more so in a social network. There's a fine line between being a peer and being a valued expert and trusted advisor. Marketing and salespeople increasingly have to straddle that line.

Peer-to-peer conversations come in a variety of different flavors. They can exist between colleagues who are working on the same project or who just work for the same company. Peer conversations take place between colleagues with similar expertise who work at different companies but have developed a professional relationship. These conversations also can exist between marketers and prospects and salespeople and buyers.

You probably already have a LinkedIn profile. If you don't, go get one; they're free. What makes LinkedIn a wealth of persona marketing information are the profiles, groups, and answers. Search for prospects by company affiliation or name. Scan their profiles for pertinent clues about their interests. Any questions they've asked or groups they belong to will be attached to their profiles, provided that they've enabled visibility. Reading their summaries and employment descriptions can provide verification that your personas are on the right track. Additionally, LinkedIn members now have the capability to pull through their blog posts, tell you what books they're reading, and provide updates about their status (almost a mini-imitation of Twitter, but not as timely).

There are a number of groups for professionals and networking and conferences organized around a myriad of topics. If you sell to CIOs, for example, joining the CIO group can expose you to discussions, thinking, and initiatives currently on their minds. Answers can be sorted by category of interest and point you to people who are asking for insights about how to solve issues, hire experts, or explore industry trends and best practices.

Even better, start a group for your prospect community on LinkedIn. HubSpot created the Pro Marketers Group, which has 19,671 opt-in members and 500 discussions underway. That's a lot of professionals with common interests talking about issues important to them. When you see a topic that captures your interest, create a newsletter that includes links to related information, and send it out to the group. Include links to your own content, but also include links to other experts' articles.

By participating in these forums, you can build your personal—as well as your company's—credibility, provided that you make sure to stay focused on the matter at hand as opposed to self-promotion or pitching your products. People will know who you are. It's on your profile. Just make sure that you're thoughtful about how you participate. Providing links to thought-leadership articles in addition to your answers also can generate awareness and prospects.

Twitter presents microcontent snacks. Because you're limited to 140 characters, you've got to be concise and on point. Providing links to articles and Web resources of interest can attract new followers and grow engagement with existing ones—as can helpful insights. Using Twitter also will make you work on clarity and succinctness in messaging—which most of us need. It's much easier to write long than short.

Don't overlook who participates on Twitter. Users could include your prospects, customers, and competitors. Tweets (Twitter posts) also tend to include some personal insights to the "Tweeter," which can help you to flesh out personas you may be struggling to complete or to verify the ones you're actively using.

Hash-tag discussions are one of the best ways to follow threads of conversations on Twitter. In fact, if you're having a Webinar, consider creating a hash-tag conversation to allow people to tweet their thoughts and questions during your presentation. You may pick up real-time additions that you can feed into the Webinar. The point is that you enable a group of people who are interested in your Webinar topic to discuss their ideas and reactions with each other in real time. By reviewing the thread afterward, you can discover new ideas, be able to gauge reactions to the material, and identify people who could be interested in buying from you.

## THE VALUE OF SOCIAL MEDIA

Measuring the impact of social media on complex sales is in its early stages. Even so, social media still can play an influential role in your marketing mix. Up-to-date research and learning more about your audiences are givens. Creating metrics for measuring value can be done in two ways. The first is to measure the increase in traffic for eMarketing content. In doing this, you will

- Monitor increased traffic generated by links to eMarketing content posted on Twitter and in LinkedIn group discussions.
- Track re-tweets by others that promote exposure and add credibility from referral value.
- Tabulate opt-ins to marketing programs resulting from all that social media–driven traffic.
- Track those prospects through to won deals.
- Track existing customer interactions to determine retention value and lifecycle impact over time.

The second metric for measuring the value of your social media initiatives focuses on engagement. Blending your social media efforts with your eMarketing strategy can serve to increase the traffic to and exposure of your content to audiences you don't know. The potential also exists to increase engagement of prospects already in your funnel when they see you in other online places they frequent. Ditto for your existing customers. Relevant content designed with calls to action will generate additional opt-ins to your content programs. When you measure engagement, you should monitor the following:

- Replies to Twitter posts
- Direct messages in Twitter from people you follow

- Answers to questions asked on LinkedIn
- Responses to discussions and news topics posted on LinkedIn
- Comments on blog posts
- Number of blog feed subscribers
- Number of back-links to your blog

Measuring engagement is not necessarily about how many followers you have on Twitter or connections you've established on LinkedIn. Indications of higher engagement can be measured by people who take action. When people take the time to respond, subscribe, or link to your content, they're demonstrating interest and verifying that you've made a connection with them. Working to improve the number and quality of the actions people take in response to your content and communications put forth through social media platforms will result in higher demand generation and get your company in more conversations that potentially can evolve into business relationships.

In marketing for complex sales, social media will produce the best results when integrated with your overall eMarketing strategy. Measurement may not be indicative of short-term revenue generation, but increased engagement will spread your ideas and expertise farther than they would ever get on their own. As you hone and tune your conversational ability and become a trusted resource, you'll find increasing business results that will tie back to social media efforts. Social media will play a starring role in the future of complex sale marketing by naturally extending the value of your nurturing programs. By embracing social media now, marketers can incrementally expand their social reach and grow participation levels within prospect communities that result in measurable company growth.

# Notes

## Chapter 2

1. Edelman Trust Barometer 2008; www.edelman.com/trust/2008/.

## Chapter 3

1. "Online Customer Engagement Report 2009," e-Consultancy with cScape, December 2008; http://econsultancy.com/reports/online-customer-engagement-report-2009.
2. "Customer Affinity: The New Measure of Marketing," CMO Council, 2007; www.cmocouncil.org/resources/form_cai_execsummary.asp.

## Chapter 4

1. "Beyond Loyalty: Meeting the Challenge of Customer Engagement," Part II, Economist Intelligence Unit, PDF report, March 2007; www.adobe.com/engagement/pdfs/partII.pdf.

## Chapter 6

1. "Business Products Buyers Survey," MarketingSherpa, Inc., March 2007.
2. "Using Assets to Drive High-Intensity Lead and Nurturing Programs," IDG, October 2008; www.idgknowledgehub.com/products/market_fusion/index.php.
3. *Ibid.*
4. Li, Charlene, and Josh Bernoff, *Groundswell: Winning in a World Transformed by Social Technologies.* Boston: Harvard Business School Publishing, 2008.

## Chapter 8

1. "Tech Target 2008 Media Consumption Benchmark Report"; www.techtarget.com/downloads/studies/TechTargetMediaConsumptionQ108.pdf.

## Chapter 9

1. Scott, David Meerman, "Gobbledygook Manifesto," August 2007; http://changethis.com/pdf/37.03.Gobbledygook.pdf.
2. Dickie, Jim, and Barry Trailer, "Keeping Up With the Buyers: The Impact of a Great First Impression," CSO Insights, July 2008; www.csoinsights.com.
3. Story, Louise. "Anywhere the Eye Can See, It's Likely to See an Ad," *New York Times*, January 15, 2007, p. 1.
4. Wilson, Deidre, and Dan Sperber. "Relevance Theory." UCL Department of Phoenetics and Linguistics, October 30, 2002; www.phon.ucl.ac.uk/home/PUB/WPL/02papers/wilson_sperber.pdf.
5. KnowlegeStorm, Inc., "Connecting Through Content: Issue One," KnowledgeStorm, March 1, 2007; www.knowledgestorm.com.
6. "Technology Vendors May Be Losing Close to 50% of Their Potential Sales Due to Inadequate Online Information," IDG, December 2008; www.idgknowledgehub.com/register/?file=Technology_Vendors_May_Be_Loosing.pdf.

## Chapter 10

1. KnowlegeStorm, Inc., "Connecting Through Content: Issue One," KnowledgeStorm, March 1, 2007; www.knowledgestorm.com.
2. "Business Products Buyers Survey," Marketing Sherpa, March 2007.

## Chapter 11

1. Wilson, Deidre, and Dan Sperber, "Relevance Theory". UCL Department of Phoenetics and Linguistics, October 30, 2002; www.phon.ucl.ac.uk/home/PUB/WPL/02papers/wilson_sperber.pdf.
2. Covey, Stephen M. R., *The Speed of Trust: The One Thing That Changes Everything*. New York: Free Press, 2006.
3. Marketing Sherpa, "Business Products Buyers Survey," March 2007.

## Chapter 12

1. Godin, Seth, Blog post: "Marketing in a Recession," February24, 2008; http://sethgodin.typepad.com/seths_blog/2008/02/marketing-in-a.html.

## Chapter 14

1. "Technology Marketing Benchmark Survey," Marketing Sherpa, Inc., April 2008.
2. Wikipedia, Serial; http://en.wikipedia.org/wiki/Serial_(literature).

## Chapter 15

1. "B-to-B Lead Generation Handbook," Marketing Sherpa, Inc., 2008.
2. "B2B Sales Lead Generation: Integration of Web 1.0 and Web 2.0 Media," Marketing Profs Research Insights, Marketing Profs, LLC, 2008; www.marketingprofs.com/store/product/14/B2B+Sales+Lead+Generation:+Integration+of+Web+1.0+and+Web+2.0+Media/1/38.
3. "B-to-B Lead Generation: Marketing ROI and Performance Evaluation Study," Marketing Profs Research Insights, Marketing Profs, LLC, 2008; www.marketingprofs.com/store/product/15/%20B2B+Lead+Generation:+Marketing+ROI+&+Performance+Evalutaion+Study.
4. "Lead Nurturing: The Secret to Successful Lead Generation," Aberdeen Group, November 2008; www.aberdeen.com/summary/report/benchmark/5378-RA-successful-lead-generation.asp.
5. *Ibid.*

## Chapter 16

1. Roche, Liz, and Jim Roche, "If Sales Effectiveness Were Baseball, the World Series Would Still Be a Few Years Away," Customers Incorporated, December 2006; http://crmguru.custhelp.com/cgi-bin/crmguru.cfg/php/enduser/std_adp.php?p_faqid=1802.
2. "One Third of Potential Selling Time Is Wasted Due to Poor Sales Enablement," IDC, November 13, 2008; www.idc.com/getdoc.jsp?containerId=prUS21519508.

## Chapter 19

1. Glazier, Bill, "Message Maps/Gaps: Making Marketing Messaging Meaningful," CMO Council, June 2004.

## Chapter 20

1. "Year-End Surveys," Marketing Sherpa, Inc., and Babcock & Jenkins, January 2009; www.marketingsherpa.com/article.php?ident=31008.

# Index

# About the Author

Ardath Albee, CEO of her firm, Marketing Interactions, Inc. is a B2B marketing strategist. She applies over 20 years of business management and marketing experience to help companies with complex sales use eMarketing strategies to generate more and better sales opportunities.

The 15 years Ardath spent serving the most demanding customers in the world as a turnaround specialist in hospitality service businesses, specifically within the resort industry, is a foundation she draws from to help companies create compelling buyer-focused content strategies.

Ardath knows that every day and every interaction is all about the customer–all the time.

When she transitioned into the technology industry in 2000, Ardath was fascinated with the disconnects she noticed in B2B companies–specifically how their intentions didn't always translate well within their marketing actions because of the often huge difference between what companies intend and their ability to translate those ideas into effective, continuous, consistent marketing and sales initiatives.

As president of a technology start-up company for more than seven years, Ardath helped companies implement marketing and sales performance software, only to see them underutilize the tools. Worse yet, Ardath also observed that companies were often unable to leverage the full capabilities of the software because they either didn't understand how to implement the changes required in the status quo and/or they didn't devote resources to the eMarketing strategies and content development requirements to best leverage the opportunities the software afforded.

In answer to this challenge, Ardath founded Marketing Interactions, Inc. to help her clients implement marketing as a strategy that reaches across the enterprise to impact all customer-facing interactions. Realizing that companies can no longer justify the lack of collaboration between marketing and sales, Ardath helps them leverage digital tools and approaches that, if used to their full potential, have a dramatic impact on streamlining sales efforts while capitalizing on business results.

Writing the Marketing Interactions blog involves Ardath in substantial industry and customer conversations, deepening her knowledge of what companies can achieve while verifying many of her marketing principles. Ardath's blog posts are referred to by other industry leaders and her blog is syndicated on community websites such as Junta42, The Customer Collective and My Venture Pad. Her articles have been used for university e-zines, and have appeared in *B2B Magazine, CRM Today, Selling Power* and *Enterprise CRM News*.

Ardath's clients include Cisco, Qwest, Silicon Graphics, and LANDesk–An Avocent Company.